Simple Projects for ClarisWorks®

Challenging

Author:

Terry Rosengart

Editor:
Evan D. Forbes, M.S. Ed.

Editorial Project Manager:
Charles Payne, M.A., M.F.A.

Editor in Chief:
Sharon Coan, M.S. Ed.

Art Director:
Elayne Roberts

Art Coordination Assistant:
Cheri Macoubrie Wilson

Product Manager:
Phil Garcia

Imaging:
Evan D. Forbes, M.S. Ed.

Acknowledgements:
ClarisWorks screen shots and clip art courtesy of Apple Computer, Inc. Used with permission.

Publishers:
Rachelle Cracchiolo, M.S. Ed.
Mary Dupuy Smith, M.S. Ed.

Teacher Created Materials

Teacher Created Materials, Inc.
6421 Industry Way
Westminster, CA 92683
ISBN-1-55690-417-2

Table of Contents

Introduction

When computers were first introduced into the classroom, we wanted our students to learn how to program them. Teachers could often be heard telling their students that they were the bosses of their computers. They were the ones who would tell the computer what to do. They were in control. A computer was nothing unless somebody directed it. We taught LOGO and BASIC. In addition to learning the way of the future, we were teaching our students how to think logically. We would be prepared for the future. We would know how to program computers.

Time passed and things changed. We realized that programming computers was a very important task, but knowing how to use one was more important. Not everybody who drove a car knew how to fix it. Not everybody who used a computer had to know how to program it. Out went programming, and in came computer assisted instruction. Now students could use computers to help them practice their subject matter. Computers were motivating ways to reinforce what had been taught in the classroom. Students would be challenged and stimulated. Work would be enriching and remedial. Computers were the future, and we were on our way there.

As with any new philosophy, time brings change. Computers are no longer the future. They are the present. They are here today, integral parts of our classrooms. While we may still teach programming and computer assisted instruction, and might still use them to reinforce subject matter, we are seeing another transition. Computers are toolboxes to use in the classroom. Each computer offers a wealth of tools to use in conjunction with classroom activities. They are as much a part of the school environment as chalkboards, pens, and books. Students are no longer limited by their school's resources. The world is theirs. They can go places without leaving the classroom. The Internet provides the highway; the computer is their vehicle.

Simple Projects for ClarisWorks is meant to serve as your guidebook to exciting curriculum centered computer activities. The projects that are presented within this book use the resources of the computer to augment your curriculum. The activities are based on content area topics in the four major curriculum areas: language arts, social studies, science, and math. Each lesson has been assigned a curriculum area, but do not let that stop you. We have integrated topics and subjects. If you are studying weather, you might want to try a math lesson that relates to hours of daylight. Writing is done within the context of social studies, language arts, and science topics.

Do not feel limited by the subject area that is included in each project. Start where we begin, but allow your creative talents, and those of your students, to flourish.

For those of you who want a cookbook—easy-to-follow directions listed in a step-by-step format—we are here for you too. Each activity is carefully spelled out. You or your students can follow the steps and complete each project with little outside help. Once your students have mastered the skills that are necessary for each activity, the step-by-step instructions will guide them along, leaving you free to work with other students on different activities.

Introduction *(cont.)*

In addition to the directions for each project, we have included work sheets, task cards, and planning pages. The work sheets that are included are meant to introduce the concepts on which some of the projects are based. Some activities include planning pages to help your students organize the information that they will use in the project. Teacher task cards are there to guide you in setting up a template file for your students to use. To make the simple projects even easier to begin, try using for each activity the templates that are found on the CD-ROM disk included with this book.

Now that the future is here and computer technology is a part of your classroom, we hope that *Simple Projects for ClarisWorks* helps you make a smooth transition in integrating technology into your curriculum. Allow the computer to work for you, and the resulting products will be fabulous.

Using This Book

As you read through *Simple Projects for ClarisWorks,* you will see pictures (icons) in the margins. They are our way of tapping you on the shoulder to give you some friendly advice. Don't ignore them. The advice is usually good and will help you along the way.

Hot Tips are not meant to burn you. They are helpful hints that will make your life easier. Once you are comfortable with *ClarisWorks*, counting the number of keystrokes that are needed to accomplish a task becomes an art. These tips will help you speed along.

How many times do you, as a teacher, say, "Did you remember to...?" Now it is our turn to say to you, "**Did 'ya?**" Take this as a friendly reminder. We would not want you to lose hours worth of work because you did not remember to save your project on a disk.

Understanding the Instructions

As you read through this book, there will be times that you are given specific instructions to follow. You might have to select an item from the menu bar, you might have to type in a specific word or name, or you might need to choose a specific button by clicking on the mouse. Use this guide for following the directions.

Instruction	What It Means
FILE	Select this pulldown menu.
italic	Select this tool from the tool bar.
Bold Italic	Make this selection from the pulldown menu.
[*file name*]	Type in this word, or this is the name of a file.
Bold	Choose this button from the dialog box.

The CD-ROM

Macintosh File Name	Windows File Name	Page
A New World	ANewWorl.CWS	58
Career Trading Cards	CareerTr.CWS	36
Clear As Glass	ClearAsG.CWS	71
Go With the Flow	GoWithth.CWS	44
Great Expectations	GreatExp.CWS	31
Homework Helper	Homework.CWS	88
How Am I Doing	HowAmIDo.CWS	79
How Loud is Loud	HowLoudi.CWS	67
In the Beginning	IntheBeg.CWS	49
Lets Talk About It	LetsTalk.CWS	54
Pattern Platter	PatternP.CWS	84
Present Your Passport	PresentY.CWS	26
Pyramid Power	PyramidP.CWS	22
Reading Relay	ReadingR.CWS	91
Sunlight Survey	Sunlight.CWS	75
Timeline to History	Timeline.CWS	13
Wanted Posters	WantedPo.CWS	7
Weather or Not	Weathero.CWS	62
Wordcross Puzzle	Wordcros.CWS	18

Following the Project Guides *(cont.)*

Each project has been divided into several components. Use this guide when explaining the activity to your students.

Title/Content Area—states the name of the project and the curriculum area it addresses.

This Project—gives a short description of the activity.

Before Beginning—explains what prior content area knowledge and planning are necessary before starting the project.

Computer Skills—explains what skills are necessary in order to complete this activity.

Quick Steps—explains the project in general terms. This is useful to the more experienced computer users.

Related Activities—are suggestions for similar projects that are appropriate for other subject areas.

Step by Step—are detailed directions that walk you through the project.

Project Sample—lets you see what the finished project might look like.

Activity Card—has short assignments that will guide your students as they work on a task.

Work Sheets—are planning pages or organizers to help your students get ready to complete their projects.

Teacher Task Card—will help you prepare a template that will be used by your students as they work on the project.

What Is a Text Makeover?

There will be times when you will be instructed to do a text makeover on the words that you have typed. This is not meant to be a one-day trip to your nearest spa; however, your printed page will come out looking like it has been refreshed. A text makeover includes changing the type of font that is used, the size of the font, and the style of the font. It is our way of telling you to make the words look special, to do something to make them look different from the rest of the text on the page.

When you are directed to do a text makeover, have fun. Explore the different possibilities. But, be cautious. If you make too many changes or make everything look special, then chances are nothing will be special. Limit your text makeovers to only select parts of your document.

Wanted Posters

This Project

In this project your students will identify key persons from history. They will explain what it is that has made this person noteworthy. What events or aspects of this person's life have made him/her somebody about whom we want to know more? Wanted Posters are a way for your students to share what they have learned about each individual with their classmates.

Computer Skills

- drawing program
- importing graphics
- changing text size, font, and style (text makeover)

Before Beginning

- Prepare a list of candidates for your Most Wanted List. Include people who are important in the history unit that your class is studying. Leave room for your students to include some people of their own choosing.
- Allow groups of two students to select the person about whom they would like to learn more.
- Students will be responsible to research pertinent information about the person whom they have chosen. This may be done independently, or you might want to allot class time for the research.
- Use the Work Sheet on page 12 to help your students organize their research.
- Use the Teacher Task Card on page 10 to create a template for this project.

Quick Steps

- Open the ClarisWorks file called *Wanted.*
- Create a text frame across the top of the page.
- After entering the selected person's name, adjust the font size to 48 points. Change the font and style so that it looks appealing to you. Center the text on the page.
- Draw a square with a 3-inch (8 cm) side just below the name. Center the square on the page. Adjust the width, pattern, and color of the square frame.
- Create another text frame beneath the square that you have just drawn. Write a short paragraph that explains who your person is and why he/she is famous. Adjust the font size to 18 points and do a text makeover.
- Place a picture in the square frame that you drew. Use the instructions on page 9 to help you place a picture in your wanted poster.
- Save the file with the person's name as the file name.
- Print a copy of your wanted poster.
- Display all of the posters on a bulletin board called *(Your school's name)'s Most Wanted List.*

Wanted Posters *(cont.)*

Step 1 Open *ClarisWorks* and click on the **Cancel** button. Pull down the **FILE** menu and select **Open**. Open the file called *Wanted.*

Step 2 Drag the mouse to the side tool bar and click the mouse button on the *Text* tool. Create a text frame by holding the mouse button down as you drag it across the page to just below the words "Wanted for Exceptional Acts."

Step 3 Type in the name of the person about whom you are making this Wanted Poster. Give your mouse button three quick clicks to highlight the line that you have just typed.

Step 4 With the name selected (highlighted), click on the **Center Alignment Control** button from the text ruler.

Step 5 Pull down the **SIZE** menu and select ***48 points*** to make the name larger.

Step 6 Pull down the **FONT** menu and choose a font that you want the name to appear in. Change the style of the name by pulling down the **STYLE** menu.

Step 7 Drag the mouse to the side tool bar and click on the *rectangle* tool. Place the crosshairs marker about 1.5 inches (3.84 cm) into the page (use the ruler to guide you). Hold the mouse button down as you drag the mouse across the page for 3 inches (8 cm). Without releasing the mouse button, drag the mouse down the page for 3 inches (8 cm). You have just drawn a square that will be the frame for the picture on your Wanted Poster.

Hold the shift key down as you draw with the rectangle tool, and you will always draw a square.

Step 8 In order to change the way this picture frame looks, the square that you drew must be selected. You know that it is selected if you see small black squares (called grabber handles) in the corners. If they are missing, click on the *pointer* arrow from the tool bar. Move the mouse so that the pointer arrow is on the square, and click the mouse button. The small boxes indicate that the square is now selected.

Step 9 Move the mouse to the *Pen Width* button in the side tool bar and hold the mouse button down. Choose a pen width that is 8 points.

Step 10 Move the mouse to the *Pen Pattern* button in the side bar and hold the mouse button down. Choose a pattern for the line.

Step 11 Move the mouse to the *Pen Color* button in the side bar and hold the mouse button down. Choose a pen color for your picture frame.

Step 12 Click on the *text* tool from the side tool bar. Drag the mouse across the page, below the picture frame. This text frame will be used to tell about the person for whom you are making this Wanted Poster. Write a short paragraph that explains who your person is and why he/she is famous. Our Wanted Posters are not meant to be used for criminals at all. We want people who are noteworthy in many different ways.

Wanted Posters *(cont.)*

Step 13 When you have proofread and spell checked your work, move the mouse so that the I-beam is in front of the first word of your paragraph. Hold the mouse button down as you drag the mouse to the end of the paragraph. The entire description should be highlighted.

Step 14 Pull down the **SIZE** menu and select ***18 points***.

Step 15 Do a text makeover to change the way the description looks.

Step 16 Add a picture into the square frame that you drew. Use the instructions at the bottom of this page to help you place a picture in your Wanted Poster.

Step 17 Pull down the **FILE** menu and select ***Save As***. Call your file the name of the person whom the poster is about. Click on the **Save** button.

Step 18 Pull down the **FILE** menu and select ***Print***. Click on the **Print** button.

Step 19 Create a bulletin board for your classroom where all of the Wanted Posters will be displayed. Make a sign for the top of the board: (Your school's name)'s Most Wanted List.

How to Add a Picture to Your Poster

If you are very artistic, you might try your hand at using the painting tools to create a portrait. Click on the *Paint* tool in the tool bar. Place the paintbrush just inside of the top left corner of the picture frame that is on the Wanted Poster. Drag the mouse to the right and down until a painting frame is inside of the picture frame. Use the painting tools to create your picture.

Look in an electronic encyclopedia or other electronic reference source for a picture of your person. Select the picture. Copy it to the computer's clipboard by pulling down the **EDIT** menu and choosing ***Copy***. Return to the Wanted Poster file and click on the *Pointer Arrow* tool. Pull down the **EDIT** menu and select ***Paste***. Move the picture to the picture frame by clicking the mouse anywhere inside of the graphic and dragging the mouse while holding the button down. Resize the picture by dragging one of its corner handles.

If you have a scanner, you can use a picture of your person that you found in a book or magazine. Use the scanner to make a digitized image of the picture. Save the scanned image according to the directions for your scanner. After you have scanned the image, open your Wanted Poster file and click on the *Pointer Arrow* tool. Pull down the **FILE** menu and select ***Insert***. Choose the file for the picture that you scanned by clicking the mouse on it. Click on the **Insert** button to place the picture in your Wanted Poster. Resize and position the graphic to fit into the picture frame that is on your poster.

If none of the above methods meets your needs, pictures can be added after the poster has been printed. Leave the space in the picture frame empty. After you have printed your Wanted Poster, paste a photocopy from a book, or an actual photograph, into the picture frame.

Wanted Posters *(cont.)*

Teacher Task Card

These instructions are designed to help you set up a template for your students to use while they are creating their own Wanted Posters. Designing this template gives consistency and uniformity to all of the Wanted Posters that your students will be creating. Their individuality will be shown in the content and form of the posters that they create.

- Open *ClarisWorks*. Click on **Drawing** to begin a new drawing document. Click on the **OK** button.
- Click on the *text* tool from the tool bar. Drag the mouse across the top of the page to create a text frame.
- Type in the word *Wanted* and press the return or enter key.
- Type in the words *for Exceptional Actions*.
- Pull down the **EDIT** menu and choose ***Select All.***
- Click on the **Center Alignment** button on the text ruler.
- Pull down the **FONT** menu and choose a font type that you like.
- Pull down the **SIZE** menu and select ***36 points***.
- Click on the *rounded rectangle* tool from the tool bar. Move the crosshairs to the top left corner of the page. Drag the mouse (while holding the button down) across the top of the page and down to the bottom right corner.
- Point the mouse on the *Paint Pattern* button at the side of the screen. Hold the mouse button down so that the paint pattern palette is displayed. Select the transparent fill pattern (two overlapping, clear boxes). With a transparent fill, the text that you have previously typed is visible once again.

If the rounded rectangle has become deselected, click on the pointer arrow, and click on the rectangle again. Remember, you can tell if an object is selected by the corner grabber boxes.

- Point the mouse on the *Pen Width* button at the side of the screen. Hold the mouse button down so that the pen width palette is displayed. Select **other** as the pen width for your page border. Type in **15** as the pen width and then click on the **OK** button.
- Point the mouse on the *Pen Pattern* button at the side of the screen. Hold the mouse button down so that the pen pattern palette is displayed. Select a pattern for the border you have placed around the edge of the screen.
- Pull down the **FILE** menu and choose ***Save As***. Type in *Wanted* as the name of the file. Click in the small circle next to the word *Stationery* and click on the **Save** button.
- The file that you have created will open as an unnamed file. When each group of students completes their Wanted Poster, the new document will need to be named. Your original file, Wanted, will remain unchanged and ready for the next group.

Wanted Posters *(cont.)*

Practice Poster

This is what your Wanted Poster will look like. Use this sample to make a Wanted Poster with your class. Select somebody from your community or school who is deserving of this award and fill in the missing information.

Wanted Posters *(cont.)*

Work Sheet

Use this page to help you organize the information that you will be using in your Wanted Poster. Use the five W's to help you gather your information.

Who is the person on your Wanted Poster? ______________________________

When in history did this person live? ______________________________

____

What did this person do that was special? ______________________________

____

____

____

Where did this person live? ______________________________

Why are this person's achievements noteworthy? ______________________________

____

____

____

With what other people or groups did this person work? ______________________________

____

____

____

____

____

What other information would make this an interesting Wanted Poster? ______________

____

____

____

____

____

Make enough copies of this work sheet so that each group can have its own planning page.

Time Line to History

This Project

In this project your students will trace a sequence of events for an historic period as they create their own time lines. This project can be customized to display experiences that relate to a specific historic era that has been studied in class. In addition to creating time lines, students are encouraged to analyze information and decide what events are worthy of inclusion.

Computer Skills

- drawing program
- manipulating text frames
- using duplicate

Before Beginning

- Select an historic event that will be used for this project. As a class, brainstorm significant events from this time period.
- Duplicate the chart on page 17 so that each computer group can have a copy of the chart.
- Form collaborative work groups of 2–3 students
- Use the Teacher Task Card on page 15 to create a template for this project.

Quick Steps

- Open the *ClarisWorks* file called *Time Line.*
- Create a text frame at the top of the screen in which you will write the title of your time line.
- Use a separate text frame to label each date on your time line. Begin with the first event on your planning sheet and end with the date for the last event. If the time line spans a long period of time, use only the year as the date.
- Draw a separate text frame for each date on your time line. Write a short description of each event that you listed in the planning sheet.
- Rotate the text frame so that the words read vertically from bottom to top. Line up each description with the corresponding date on the time line.
- Save your file with the name *Time Line* for your topic.
- Print a copy of your time line.

Time Line to History *(cont.)*

Step 1 Open *ClarisWorks* and click on the **Cancel** button. Pull down the **FILE** menu and select ***Open***. Open the file called *Time Line*.

Step 2 Click on the *text* tool from the tool bar. Drag the mouse across the top of the screen to form a text frame.

When you select the *text* tool from the tool bar, double-click on it. This will make the selected tool the default value (whenever you need a new tool, the double-clicked tool will automatically be selected). Since we are going to use a lot of text frames now, this is a handy timesaver.

Step 3 Type in the title of your time line. It should be related to the historical event that you are discussing.

Step 4 Use a separate text frame to label each date on your time line. Begin with the first event on your planning sheet and end with the date for the last event. If the time line spans a long period of time, use only the year as the date. Since you have previously double-clicked on the text tool, you do not have to select it at this time.

Step 5 Draw another text frame at any available place on the screen.

Step 6 Begin with the first event on your planning sheet and write a short description of the event.

Step 7 Follow steps 5 and 6 to create short descriptions for each event that you listed in your planning chart.

Step 8 Click on the *Pointer Arrow* from the tool bar. Click the mouse button when the arrow is pointing to one of the event descriptions. This text frame is now selected.

Step 9 Pull down the **ARRANGE** menu and select ***Free Rotate***. Notice how the pointer arrow is now an "X." Place the "X" on the top right grabber handle of the selected text frame and slowly move the mouse (with the button depressed) in a circular motion. The text frame will rotate as the mouse moves. Continue until the words can be read vertically from bottom to top.

Step 10 Repeat Step 9 to rotate each of the text frames. Line up each description with the corresponding date on the time line.

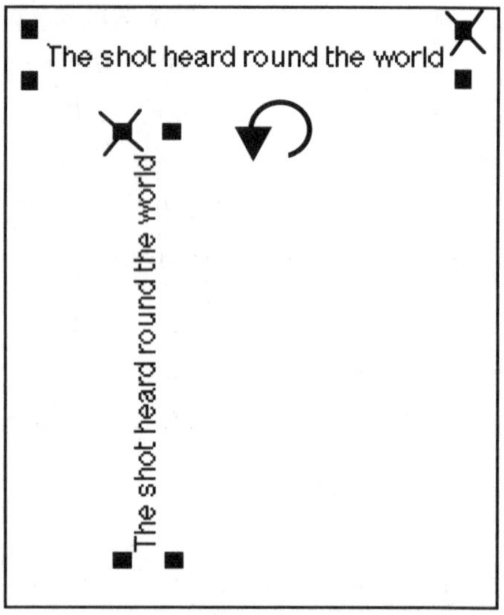

Step 11 Pull down the **FILE** menu and select ***Save As***. Name your file *Time Line* for your topic. Click on the **Save** button.

Step 12 Pull down the **FILE** menu and select ***Print***. Click on the **Print** button to print your time line.

Time Line to History *(cont.)*

Teacher Task Card

These instructions are designed to help you set up a template for your students to use while they are creating their own Time Lines.

- Open a new *ClarisWorks* document. Click on **Drawing** and then select **OK**.
- Pull down the **FILE** menu and choose ***Page Setup***. Click on the landscape icon next to Orientation. Your page is set so that it will lie sideways.
- Click on the *line* tool from the tool bar. Point the mouse to the **line width** button and hold down the mouse button. Choose an ***8-point*** line.
- Move the crosshairs to the left margin of the page and drag the mouse across the screen to the right margin. Holding the shift key down as you drag the mouse will give you a straight line.
- Click on the *line* tool again. This time, you will be drawing short, vertical lines along the vertical line that you just made. Set this line width to ***2 points***.
- Move the crosshairs so that they are at the beginning of the time line. Draw a straight line that goes up .5 inch (1.3 cm).

If you do not have rulers on your screen, pull down the **VIEW** menu and select ***Show Rulers***. If you do not have graphics rulers (on the side and top of the screen), pull down the **FORMAT** menu and select ***Rulers***. Click in the circle next to ***Graphic*** and then click on **OK**. You can set the rulers to inches or centimeters.

- With the marker line still selected, pull down the **EDIT** menu and choose ***Duplicate***. Move the second marker line to a spot one inch (2.5 cm) to the right of the first marker. Evenly spaced markers will appear with each duplicate that you select. Continue to select ***Duplicate*** from the **EDIT** menu until the entire time line has markers.
- Pull down the **FILE** menu and choose ***Save As***. Type in *Time Line* as the name of the file. Click in the small circle next to the word Stationery and click on the **Save** button.
- The file that you have created will open as an unnamed file. When each group of students completes their Time Line, the new document will need to be named. Your original file, Time Line, will remain unchanged and ready for the next group to use.

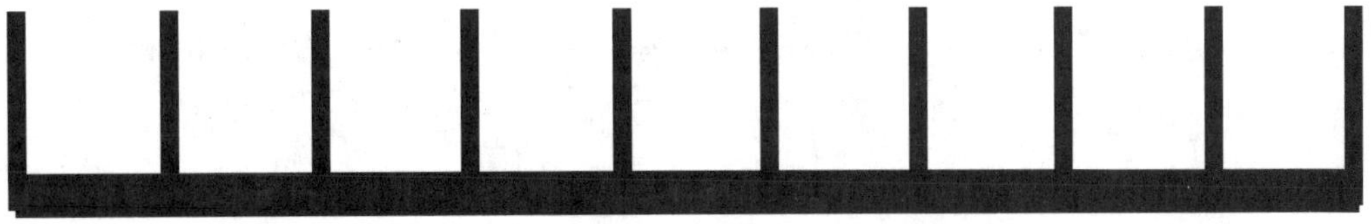

Time Line to History *(cont.)*

Sample Time Line

This is what your Time Line to History will look like. Use this sample to practice making a Time Line as a class. Create a Time Line that indicates what a day in school looks like for your class.

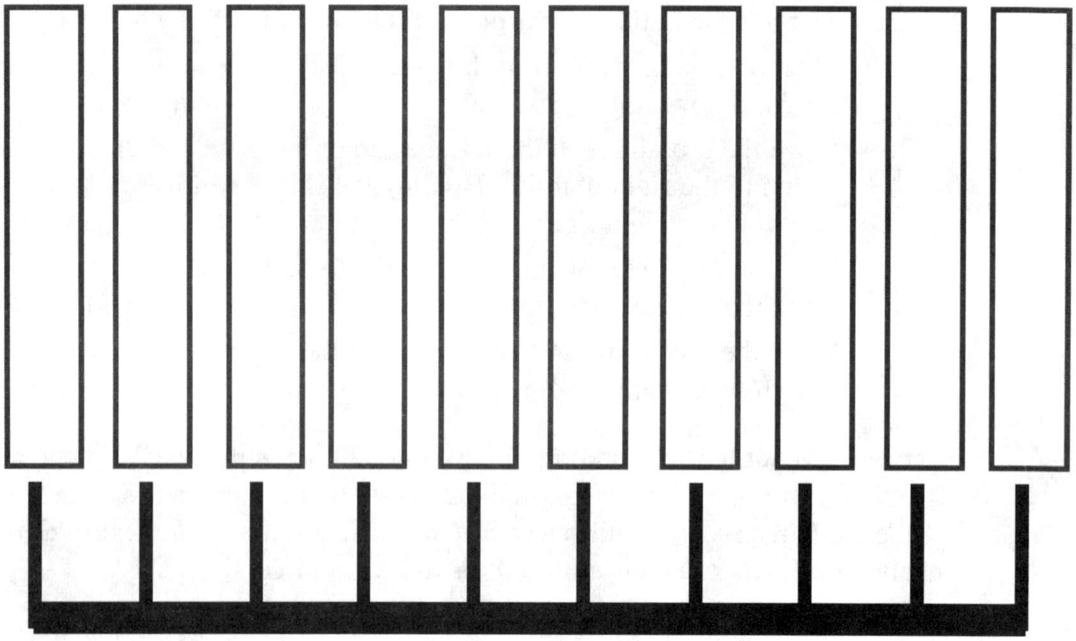

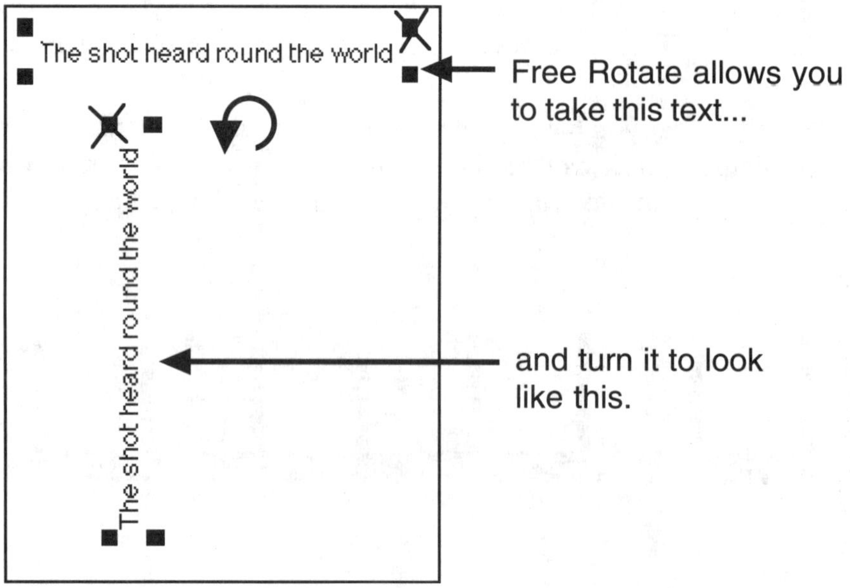

Time Line to History *(cont.)*

Work Sheet

This chart will help you organize the information that will be included in your Time Line. Copy the events that your class has listed for this historical event. Use your textbook and other reference materials to find the dates on which these events occurred.

Timeline Planning Chart

Topic ______________________________

Prepared by ____________________________ Class ______________

Event	**Date**

Make enough copies of this work sheet so that each group can have its own chart.

Wordcross Puzzle

This Project

This project allows your students to review material that they have learned. They are given the answers, and their job is to write the questions. Using a crossword puzzle format that displays key words and phrases from your social studies unit, students are given the task to write the clues that will generate the given answers.

Computer Skills

- spreadsheet
- adding text frames
- resizing cells

Before Beginning

- For this activity, the teacher can follow the step-by-step directions on the Teacher Task Card on page 20 to prepare his/her own puzzle for students to complete, or the class can be divided into two groups. One group will construct the puzzle while the other fills in the missing clues.
- Bring in samples of crossword puzzles for your class to examine. Discuss how one usually completes a crossword puzzle and explain how in this case, the answers are given, and the user needs to write the clues.
- Select a topic that your class has been studying and prepare a list of ten important words or phrases.
- Complete the sample wordcross puzzle on page 21 as practice before beginning this project on the computer.

Quick Steps

- Open the file called *Wordcross.*
- Create a text frame below the puzzle. Stretch the text frame so that it covers half of the width of the screen. Type the word *Across.*
- Starting at the top left corner of the puzzle, write the cell address of the first cell of each word or phrase that goes across the grid. Write each cell address on a new line.
- When the first row is finished, move to the second row of the grid. Continue until the first cell of each *Across* word has been noted.
- Create a text frame to the right of the first text frame. Stretch the text frame so that it covers the right half of the screen. Type the word *Down.*
- Starting at the top left corner of the puzzle, write the cell address of the first cell of each word or phrase that goes down the grid. Write each cell address on a new line.
- When the first column is finished, move to the second column of the grid. Continue until the first cell of each *Down* word has been noted.
- Write a clue next to each cell address that describes the word or phrase that begins in that cell.
- Save the file with the file name *Wordcross Puzzle.*
- Print a copy of your completed Wordcross Puzzle.

Wordcross Puzzle *(cont.)*

Step 1 Open *ClarisWorks* and click on the **Cancel** button. Pull down the **FILE** menu and select ***Open***. Open the file called *Wordcross*.

Step 2 Click on the *text* tool from the tool bar. Hold down the mouse button as you drag the mouse beneath the puzzle, forming a text frame that extends halfway across the screen. Type the word *Across* into the text frame. Do a text makeover on the word.

Step 3 Look at the puzzle and find the first word or phrase (from the top left corner) that is going across the grid. Identify the cell address of the first letter of that word. For example, in the sample on page 21, the phrase "Public Works Administration" begins in cell A4. Press the return or enter key to move to a new line.

Step 4 Look in each row of the puzzle for the first cell of each word. Continue to list the cell address of the first letter of each word, remembering to move to a new line for each cell address. Continue until the first cell of each *Across* word has been noted.

Step 5 Click on the *text* tool in the side toolbar. Drag the mouse while holding down the mouse button to create another text frame to the right of the previous one. Type in the word *Down* into this text frame. Change the font to look like the font in the word "Across."

Step 6 Look at the puzzle and find the first word or phrase (from the top left corner) that is going down the grid. Identify the cell address of the first letter of that word. For example, in the sample on page 21, the phrase "Collective Bargaining" begins in cell F4. Press the return or enter key to move to a new line.

Step 7 Look in each column of the puzzle for the first cell of each word. Continue to list the cell address of the first letter of each word, remembering to move to a new line for each cell address. Continue until the first cell of each *Down* word has been noted.

Step 8 Move the mouse until the I-beam is next to the first cell address in the Across column. Click the mouse button to place the cursor at that spot. Type in a clue that describes the word that begins in that cell.

Step 9 Move the mouse to place the I-beam after the next cell address in the Across column. Write another clue.

Remember to click the mouse button, or the cursor will not be placed in this new location.

Step 10 Repeat Steps 8 and 9 until you have written clues for all of the cell addresses that you have listed.

Step 11 Pull down the **FILE** menu and select ***Save As***. Name your file *Wordcross Puzzle*. Click on the **Save** button.

Step 12 Pull down the **FILE** menu and select ***Print***. Click on the **Print** button to print your completed Wordcross Puzzle.

Wordcross Puzzle *(cont.)*

Teacher Task Card

Use these directions to create a Wordcross Puzzle. You can prepare the puzzle yourself or have groups of students work together to form their own puzzles.

Before you begin to work at the computer, prepare a list of ten words or phrases that you want to use for your Wordcross Puzzle.

Step 1 Open a new *ClarisWorks* document. Click on **Spreadsheet** and then click on the **OK** button.

Step 2 Find the longest word or phrase from your word list. This will be the first answer that you will place in the puzzle. (Looking at the sample puzzle on page 21; the first phrase was "Public Works Administration.") These words will be placed in the puzzle, one letter at a time. Do not leave blank spaces between words.

Step 3 Move the mouse until the pointer arrow is in cell A4. Click the mouse button to make this the active cell.

Step 4 Type the first letter of the word or phrase into cell A4. Press the tab key. This moves the letter that you have typed from the entry bar to the active cell. At the same time, using the tab key makes the next cell in the row the new active cell.

Step 5 Repeat Step 4 as you type each letter of the word or phrase. Once you have developed a rhythm of typing a letter and then pressing the tab key, entering each word or phrase will go smoothly.

Step 6 Look for another long word or phrase. Place these letters going down in a column. Try to find a location where the vertical word lines up with one of the letters near the beginning of the first word. (In the sample puzzle, the words "Collective Bargaining" were lined up with the first phrase.) The common letter can be the first, second, or third letter of this word.

Step 7 Move the mouse until the pointer arrow is in the cell where you want to place the first letter. Click the mouse button to make this the active cell.

Step 8 Type the first letter of the word or phrase into the selected cell. Press the return or enter key. This moves the letter that you have typed from the entry bar to the active cell. At the same time, using the return or enter key makes the next cell in the column the new active cell.

Step 9 Repeat Step 8 as you type each letter of the word or phrase. Once you have developed a rhythm of typing a letter and then pressing the return or enter key, entering each word or phrase will go quickly.

Step 10 Continue this process as you place each of your words into the grid.

Step 11 Pull down the **FILE** menu and select ***Save As***. Type in the file name, *Wordcross*. Click the small circle next to the word Stationery and then click on the **Save** button.

The file that you have created will open as an unnamed file. When each group of students completes its Wordcross Puzzle, the new document will need to be named. Your original file, Wordcross, will remain unchanged and ready for the next group to use.

Wordcross Puzzle *(cont.)*

Work Sheet

Use this sample Wordcross Puzzle to practice writing clues. From what period of time in American history do these answers come?

	A	B	C	D	E	F	G	H	I	J	K	L	M	N	O	P	Q	R	S	T	U	V	W	X	Y
1	The Great Depression																								
2																									
3																									
4	P	U	B	L	I	C	W	O	R	K	S	A	D	M	I	N	I	S	T	R	A	T	I	O	N
5						O																			
6					B	L	A	C	K	T	U	E	S	D	A	Y									
7						L																			
8						E																			
9						C	O	N	S	U	M	E	R												
10						T									U										
11					M	I	G	R	A	N	T				N										
12						V								N	E	W	D	E	A	L					
13						E									M										
14		D	U	S	T	B	O	W	L						P										
15						A									L										
16	H	O	O	V	E	R	V	I	L	L	E	S			O										
17						G									Y										
18						A									M										
19						I									E										
20						N									N										
21			S	O	C	I	A	L	S	E	C	U	R	I	T	Y									
22						N																			
23						G																			

ACROSS

A4

E6

F9

E11

N12

B14

A16

C21

DOWN

F4

O10

Make enough copies of this work sheet so that each student can have his/her own chart.

Pyramid Power

This Project

Use this project to help your students visualize the important information that they have learned from their studies about modern and ancient Egypt. Groups of students will construct pyramids whose bricks contain vital facts about this country. After the pyramids have been printed and displayed, comparisons of the ancient and modern civilizations can be made.

Computer skills

- drawing
- text frames
- fill and pen patterns and colors

Before Beginning

- This project is an activity that is best used as your class studies Egypt (both past and present). The pyramid that they will be building on the computer will grow as your class acquires more information. As a class, prepare a chart containing facts that might be included in the pyramid. This information might be gathered from your textbook or through individual research.
- Prepare a semantic map that organizes the above information into general categories. These topics might include the following: Housing, Cities, Rulers, Culture, Customs, Time Line, Geography.

Quick Steps

- Open a new *ClarisWorks* drawing program
- Draw a large triangle in the center of the screen. Make the pen width ***8 points***. Select a fill pattern and color for this object.
- Line the base of the triangle with a row of four rectangles (bricks).
- Align the shapes so that they form a straight row.
- Add another row above it that contains three bricks. Continue building up until there is one brick in the row.
- Change the pen pattern and color for each row.
- Add a text frame to each brick.
- Enter a fact about ancient Egypt in each block. Each layer (row) should contain information from the same general category.
- Save the file with the file name *Ancient Pyramid Power*.
- Repeat this process to create a second pyramid. Fill this one with information about modern Egypt.
- Save the file with the file name *Modern Egypt*.
- Print one copy each of both pyramids.

Pyramid Power *(cont.)*

Step 1 Open *ClarisWorks* and select **Drawing**. Click on the **OK** button.

Step 2 Move the pointer arrow to the *regular polygon* tool on the tool bar. Click the mouse button to select it.

Step 3 Pull down the **OPTIONS** menu and select ***Polygon Sides***. Change the number of sides to be three. Click on the **OK** button.

Step 4 Drag the mouse across the screen until the triangle that is drawn occupies most of the area. While still holding down the mouse button, rotate the triangle so that the base is flat at the bottom of the screen.

You can also adjust the way the triangle is sitting on the page by selecting ***Free Rotate*** from the **ARRANGE** menu. A small X replaces the pointer arrow. Position this pointer on one of the corner handles and drag the mouse to rotate the placement of the triangle. When you are finished rotating the object, click on ***Free Rotate*** again to deselect it.

Step 5 With the triangle still selected, click on the pen width palette and choose ***8 points***.

Step 6 Click on the fill pattern palette and choose a brick pattern to fill the triangle.

Step 7 Click on the fill color palette and select a color for the triangle.

Step 8 Click on the *rectangle* tool from the tool bar. Draw a rectangle that is about 2.5 inches (6.3 cm) wide and 1 inch (2.5 cm) high. Drag this rectangle so that it is placed in the bottom left corner of the triangle.

Step 9 Pull down the **EDIT** menu and choose ***Copy***.

Step 10 Pull down the **EDIT** menu and select ***Paste***. Drag the new rectangle so that it is in line next to the first one. Continue pasting until there is a row of four rectangular bricks along the bottom edge of the triangle.

Step 11 Select the *Pointer Arrow* from the tool bar. Hold the shift key down as you click the pointer arrow on each rectangle.

Step 12 Pull down the **ARRANGE** menu and select ***Align Objects***. Click in the circle next to Align Top Edges. Click on the **OK** button.

Step 13 With the four rectangles still selected, pull down the **ARRANGE** menu and choose ***Group***. The four rectangles are now treated as one object. Drag the entire row of bricks until it is placed neatly at the bottom of the triangle.

Pyramid Power *(cont.)*

Step 14 Pull down the **EDIT** menu and select ***Paste***. Drag the rectangle so that it is above the bottom row of bricks. Paste two more bricks.

Step 15 Line up the three bricks next to each other. Repeat steps 11–13 to form a row of three bricks that are above the bottom row.

Step 16 Continue building up the pyramid until there is one brick at the top.

Step 17 Click on the *pointer arrow* tool and select one of the rows. Click on the pen palette and change the size of the line to ***4 point***s. Select a pen pattern for this row.

Step 18 Change the pen pattern and size for each row of bricks.

Step 19 Click on the *text* tool in the tool bar. Drag the mouse so that a text frame is drawn in one of the bricks. Enter a fact about ancient Egypt in that block.

Step 20 Continue to enter information into each block, remembering to draw a text frame first. Each layer (row) of the pyramid should contain information from the same general category.

Step 21 Pull down the **FILE** menu and select ***Save As***. Give the file the name *Ancient Pyramid Power*.

Step 22 Pull down the **FILE** menu and select ***Print***. Click on the **Print** button.

Step 23 Repeat this process to create another pyramid. This time use information that you know about modern Egypt. Give this file the file name *Modern Egypt*.

Step 24 Print a copy of the Modern Egypt pyramid. Display both pyramids next to each other. What similarities do you see? What are the differences between ancient Egypt and the Egypt that we know from modern times?

Pyramid Power *(cont.)*

Sample Page

Use this sample pyramid to help you organize your ideas. What general category will each row contain? What information do you want to place in each brick?

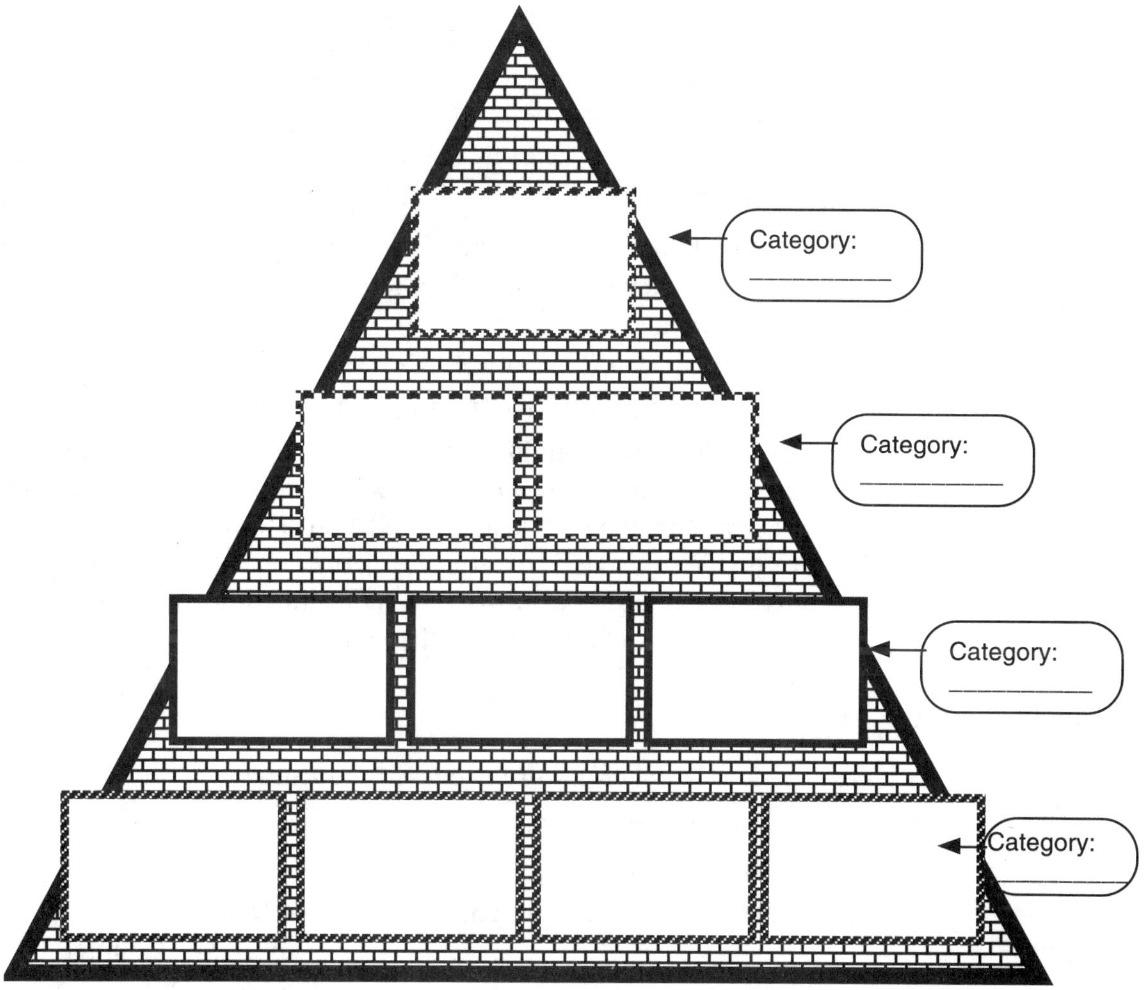

Make enough copies of this work sheet so that each student can have his/her own planning page.

Present Your Passport

This Project

In this project your students will design passports from a country or geographic region that they have studied. They will include information about each country in its passport, including such facts as population, area, type of government, and capital.

Computer Skills

- word processing
- working with columns
- font makeovers

Before Beginning

- Your students should understand the various facts that will be listed on each passport. Use the chart on page 30 to identify and explain what information will be needed for each category.
- Divide the class into groups of two for this project. Assign each group a country for which they will create a passport.
- Each group of students should complete the Planning Page on page 30 with information about the country that has been assigned to them. Students might find the necessary facts in an atlas, a CD-ROM atlas, online, using the World Wide Web. A good Web site to look at is *The World Factbook.* Go to **www.odci.gov/cia/publications/nsolo/wfb-all.htm** to find some interesting information about every country in the world.

Quick Steps

- Open a new *ClarisWorks* word processing document.
- Make the page setup landscape.
- Choose a two-column page.
- Make a text frame in the right column. Type—*Passport*
  Name of Country
  Issued to
  Your Name
- Do a font makeover and center the text on the page.
- Insert a page break.
- Use the left column of page two to discuss information about the country, including facts and events from its history.
- Use the right column on page two to explain what sights there are to see and things there are to do in this country.
- Do a text makeover for this text.
- Put a border around each column of both pages.
- Save the file with the file name *Passport.*

Present Your Passport *(cont.)*

Step 1 Open *ClarisWorks* and click on ***Word Processing***. Click on the **OK** button.

Step 2 Pull down the **FILE** menu and select ***Page Setup***. Click on the **Landscape** icon so that the page is displayed with the long side in its width.

Step 3 Click on the **Increase Column** button until there are ***two columns***.

Step 4 Click on the *text* tool in the tool bar. Move the mouse so that the I-beam is in the column on the right. Hold the option key down as you drag the mouse across the column, holding the mouse button down at the same time. This creates a text frame.

When you are working in a word processing document there are times that you will want to create a separate text frame. Unlike the regular writing area of a word processing document, this process allows you to select and drag the text to wherever you want it to be. You can also resize a text frame to modify the width of the area that the text occupies. Holding the option key down as you drag the I-beam across a space creates a separate text frame.

Step 5 Click on the **Center Alignment** button on the text ruler.

Step 6 Type the word *Passport* and press the return or enter key.

Step 7 Type the name of the country for which you are designing this passport and then press return or enter.

Step 8 Type the words *Issued to* and press return or enter.

Step 9 Enter your name on the next line.

Step 10 Do a text makeover on these words. They should be a large font size (**SIZE** menu). The country and your name should be in an even larger size.

Step 11 Change the type of letters (**FONT** menu) and the way they look (**STYLE** menu).

Step 12 Click on the **Zoom Percentage Box** and adjust the percentage to ***50%***.

Step 13 Use the *pointer arrow* from the tool bar to select the text frame. Drag the selected frame down the page until the text is in the middle of the space for the right column.

Step 14 Click on the **Zoom Percentage Box** and adjust the percentage to ***100%***.

Step 15 Move the mouse until the I-beam is in the top left corner of the screen. Click the mouse button to place the cursor there.

Step 16 Pull down the **FORMAT** menu and choose ***Insert Page Break***. This will bring you to the top of page two.

Step 17 Follow Step 4 to create a text frame in the left column. In this space write about the country. You can use a straight narrative form, an outline format, or bullets to highlight specific points. Tell the facts that you learned about this country. Explain significant aspects of the country's history.

Present Your Passport *(cont.)*

Step 18 Create a text frame in the column on the right by following the directions in Step 4. Use this area to tell what one would see and do when visiting this country.

Step 19 Do a font makeover on the text in both columns. Make the headings and titles look special.

Step 20 Select the *Rounded Rectangle* tool from the tool bar. Move the crosshairs to the top left corner of the right column on the first page. Hold down the mouse button as you drag the mouse across the column and down the page.

Step 21 With the rectangular frame that you just drew still selected, click on the **Line Width** palette and choose ***8 points***.

Step 22 Click on the **Line Pattern** palette and select a pattern that you like.

Step 23 Click on the **Fill Pattern** palette and choose the ***Transparent*** fill pattern.

Step 24 Pull down the **EDIT** menu and select ***Copy***.

Step 25 Pull down the **EDIT** menu and choose ***Paste***.

Step 26 Drag the second rectangular frame to the second page, placing it on the text in the left column.

Step 27 Repeat Steps 25 and 26 for the right column on the second page.

Step 28 Pull down the **FILE** menu and choose ***Save As***. Give the file the name *Passport*. Click on the **Save** button.

Step 29 Pull down the **FILE** menu and choose ***Print***. When the dialog box appears, click in the box next to the word "From:" and type the number *1*. Now click in the box next to the word "To:" and type in the number *1*. This tells the computer to print only page one of your document. Click on the **Print** button.

Step 30 Take the page that was just printed, and reinsert it into the printer. Place the page facedown with the top of the paper (the left column) nearest to the printer.

Step 31 Repeat Step 29, only this time, print **From** page 2 **To** page 2.

Practice printing on both sides of the page before you try the real one. It is better to see how this is done on a document that you do not need than to make a mistake on the real thing.

Present Your Passport *(cont.)*

Printing on Two Sides of a Page

- Print the first page of the document.
- Take the printed paper and put it back into the printer facedown with the top of the paper nearest to the printer.

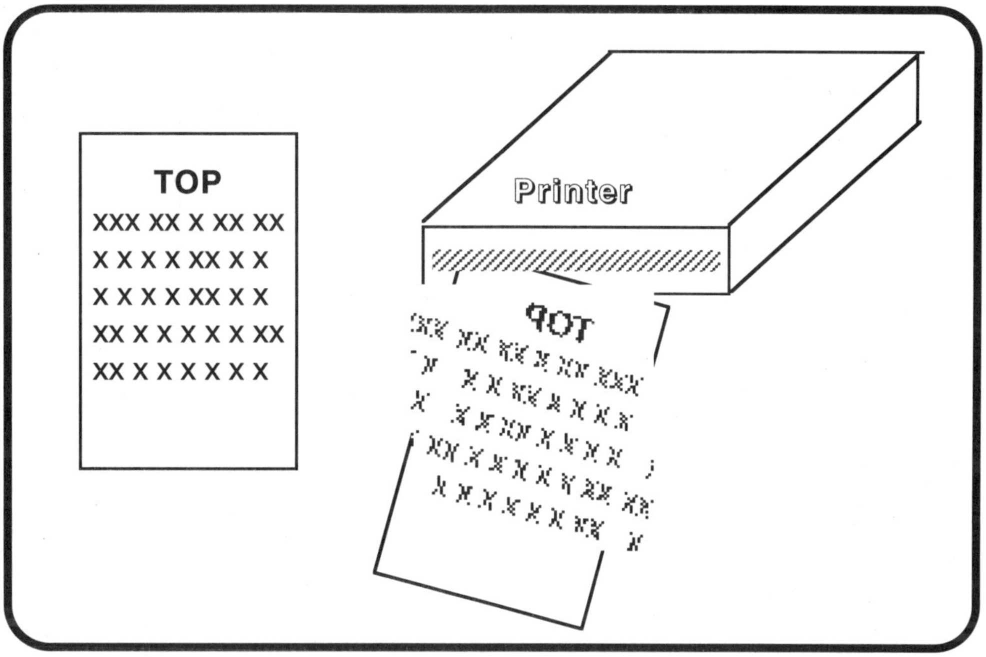

- Print the second page of the document.

Present Your Passport (cont.)

Planning Page

Use this chart to prepare you for creating your own passports. As a class, fill in the information as it pertains to your own country. Where can you locate these facts?

Name of Country	
Continent	
Population	Flag
Area	
Form of Government	
Current leader	
Language spoken	
Historic Events	
Places to Visit	
Things to Do	

Learn more about another country. Place the information into this chart. When you have gathered enough information, design a passport, following the instructions in ***Present Your Passport***.

Name of Country	
Continent	
Population	Flag
Area	
Form of Government	
Current leader	
Language spoken	
Historic Events	
Places to Visit	
Things to Do	

Make enough copies of this work sheet so that each group can have its own copy.

Great Expectations

This Project

Get your students thinking technology from the very beginning of the school year. In this project students will design and make entries in their own double-entry journals. Their anticipations of what they want to learn and accomplish during the school year will be compared to what has actually been accomplished. This project begins in September and concludes at the end of the school year.

Computer Skills

- word processing
- using columns
- text makeovers

Before Beginning

- As a class, brainstorm what will make this school year different from the previous one. Along with different curriculum, there are sure to be other activities or responsibilities that will change. What rights and privileges do students in your grade have that were not available in previous years? What curriculum projects can they look forward to? What special trips and activities will they experience? "Wow" them from the start, and they will be eager for the remainder of the year.
- Complete the K-W-L chart on page 35 to help your students organize their thoughts.

Quick Steps

- Open a new *ClarisWorks* word processing document.
- Format the page with two columns.
- Create a text frame across the top of the page for the title, *Great Expectations*. Use an 18-point font.
- Use a 14-point font to write the heading for the left column, *What I Expect*.
- Use a 14-point font to write the heading for the right column, *What Actually Happened*.
- Do a font makeover on the column headings and the page title.
- Change to a regular, 12-point font and write a short paragraph about a few things that you think will happen this school year. Title each idea.
- Do a font makeover for each title.
- Save your file with the name *Great Expectations*.
- At the end of the school year, open the *Great Expectations* file.
- In the right column, next to each entry, write a short paragraph about what actually happened.
- Save and print your Great Expectations chart.

Great Expectations *(cont.)*

Step 1 Open *ClarisWorks*. Select **Word Processing** and then click on the **OK** button.

Step 2 Move the mouse so that the pointer arrow is on the column buttons in the text ruler at the top of the screen. Click one time on the button with two columns, dividing your page into two columns. Notice how the number 2 appears, indicating that your page now has two columns.

Step 3 Move the mouse to the tool bar and click on the *text* tool. Hold down the option key as you drag the mouse across the top of the screen, creating a text frame across the two columns.

When you are creating a word processing document with columns and you want to write past the column boundaries, you need to make a text frame that defines where you will enter the text. Holding the option key as you drag the mouse (after the *text* tool has been selected) lets you create a text frame and write where you want to.

Step 4 Type in the title for this page, *Great Expectations*.

Step 5 Highlight the title line by clicking the mouse button on it three times. Pull down the **SIZE** menu and select ***18 point***. Do a font makeover for the title.

Step 6 Click on the **Center Align** button to center the text on the page.

Step 7 Move the mouse so that the pointer arrow is at the top of the left column. Click the mouse button to place the cursor. Press the return or enter key a few times to move the cursor to a spot that is below the title.

Step 8 Click on the **Center Align** button and type *What I Expect*.

Step 9 Highlight the column heading by dragging your mouse across the words and pull down the **SIZE** menu. Select ***14 point***. Do a font makeover for the column heading.

Step 10 Pull down the **FORMAT** menu and choose ***Insert Column Break***. The cursor is now at the top of the right column. Press the return or enter key a few times to move the cursor down to the line that matches the left column heading.

Step 11 Click on the **Center Align** button and type *What Actually Happened*.

Step 12 Highlight the column heading by dragging your mouse across the words and pull down the **SIZE** menu. Select ***14 point***. Do a font makeover for this column heading.

Step 13 Repeat Step 12 for the right column. Remember to highlight the words that you want to make over.

Step 14 Move the mouse so that the pointer arrow is at the end of the left column heading. Click the mouse button to place it there. Press the return or enter key two times to move the cursor down two lines.

Great Expectations *(cont.)*

Step 15 Pull down the **SIZE** menu and choose ***12 point***.

Step 16 Pull down the **STYLE** menu and select ***Plain Text***.

Step 17 Write a short paragraph about a few things that you think will happen during this school year. Include a title for each idea.

Step 18 Highlight the title of your first topic. Do a font makeover for each topic. Make all of the topic headings look alike.

Step 19 Pull down the **FILE** menu and select ***Save As***. Give the file the name *Great Expectation*s and click on the **Save** button.

Keep this file safely stored on your data disk until the end of the school year. We will revisit it as summer vacation nears. When you are ready to resume working on this file, follow these steps:

Step 20 Open *ClarisWorks* and click on the **Cancel** button.

Step 21 Pull down the **FILE** menu and select ***Open***. Find the title of your file, *Great Expectations*. Click on it and then click on the **Open** button.

Step 22 Move the mouse to the right column so that the I-beam is after the title, *What Actually Happened*. Click the mouse button to place it there. Press the return or enter key until the cursor is in line with the text in the left column. Write a short paragraph about what actually happened during this school year. Include your reactions and analysis along with the facts.

Step 23 Press the return or enter key until the cursor is in line with the second topic. Write an update for that topic. Continue until you have responded to all topics.

Step 24 Pull down the **FILE** menu and select ***Save As***. Click on the **Save** button. When asked if you want to replace the existing file, click on the **Replace** button.

Step 25 Pull down the **FILE** menu and select ***Print***. Click on the **Print** button to print a hard copy of your Great Expectations chart. Did your school year turn out the way that you had hoped it would?

Great Expectations *(cont.)*

Sample Page

This is what your Great Expectations page will look like. Be careful when you add text to the right column. Each topic should line up with the entry in the left column.

After entering text in the right column, you may find that you need to adjust your entries in the left column.

- Use the return or enter key to move the text down a few lines.
- Use the delete key to move the text up a few lines.

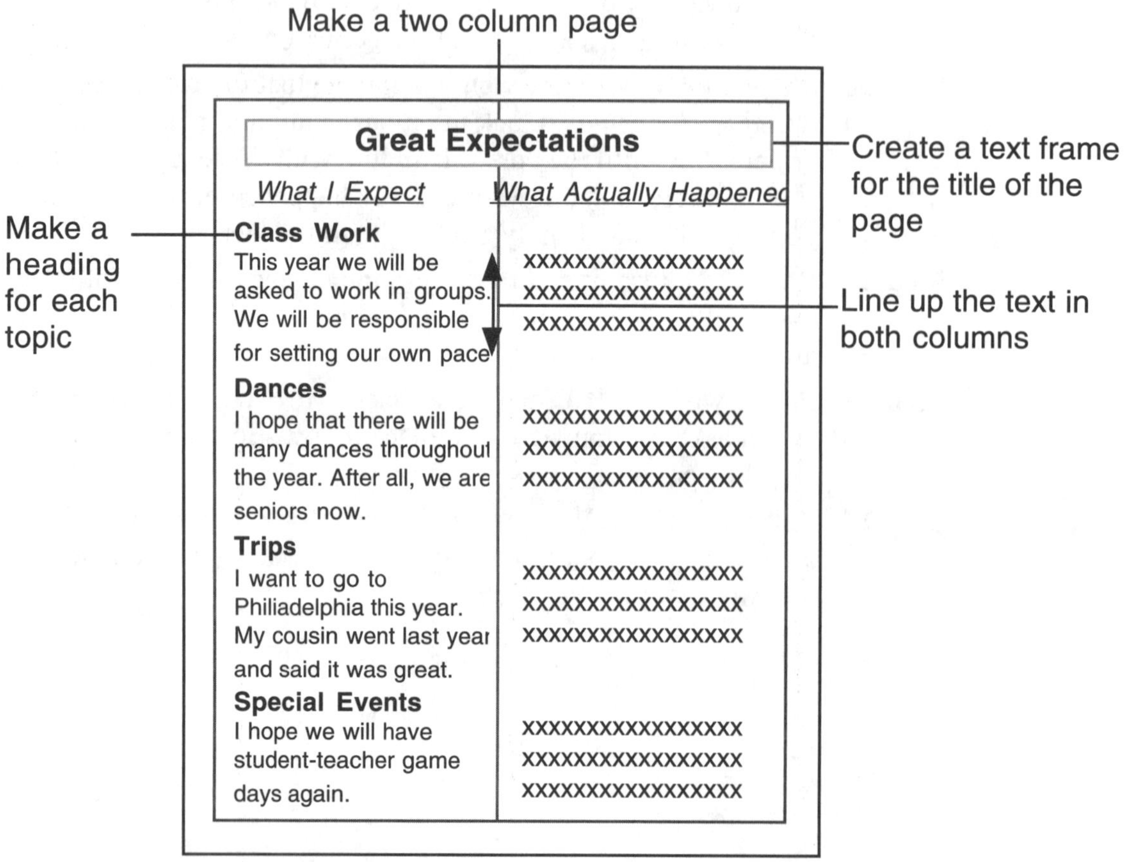

Great Expectations *(cont.)*

Student Work Sheet

A K-W-L chart is used to help you organize your thoughts. The first column contains information that you already **K**now. The second column is for the information that you **W**ant to learn. The last column is used to show what you have actually **L**earned.

In the beginning of this school year, you can complete only the first two columns. Save this paper so that you can finish the last column before summer vacation.

- Use the information that your class has brainstormed to add items to the first two columns.
- At the end of the school year, add items to column three. Tell about things that happened during the year.

What I KnowAbout This Year	What I Think Will Happen This Year	What Actually Did Happen This Year

Make enough copies of this work sheet so that each student can have his/her own planning page.

Career Trading Cards

This Project

In this project your students will explore career opportunities as they create their own trading cards. The front side of each card will contain the student's picture and biographical information. The flip side will hold facts relating to a career that the student has selected. Each student will receive several copies of his/her own card which can be swapped during a card trading day.

- drawing
- using text frames
- inserting graphics

Computer Skills

Before Beginning

- As a class, discuss what type of trading cards your students have seen, e.g., baseball, hockey, music, t.v. shows. Students might want to bring in some samples from their own collections. Elicit from the class what items would be important to include on a trading card.
- Distribute copies of the Biography Work Sheet on page 41. Each student will complete his/her own planning page.
- Discuss the importance of career awareness and setting career goals. Each student should select a career about which he/she would like to learn more. They may research it in any way that they want, but in the end, they should have enough information to complete the Career Work Sheet on page 42.
- Follow the step-by-step directions on the Teacher Task Card on page 39 to prepare the template that will be used to create the trading cards.
- Each student will need a digitized photo of his/herself to place on the card. These pictures can come from several sources. Use the guide on page 43 to find the best choice for you.

Quick Steps

- Open the file called *Trading Cards.*
- All work will be done in the top left rectangle guide. Leaving a .25 inch (.6 cm) margin between the text frame and the side and bottom edges of the card, draw a text frame that begins 1/3 of the way down the card and stretches across the card.
- Type in your name. Give it a center alignment. Do a text makeover on the words.
- Select the information that you want to include about yourself and type it below your name.
- Insert your photograph in the empty space at the top of the card. Resize the picture to fit into the available area.
- Draw a border around the outside of the card.
- After you have proofread and checked all items, select and copy all of the objects from the card.
- Paste these items into the remaining eight rectangle guides.
- Move to page 2 of the file.
- Leaving a .25 inch (.6 cm) margin between the text frame and all of the edges of the card, draw a text frame that stretches across and down the card.

Career Trading Cards *(cont.)*

Step 1 Open *ClarisWorks* and click on the **Cancel** button. Pull down the **FILE** menu and select ***Open***. Find the file called "Trading Cards" and click on it to select it. Click on the **Open** button.

The file that you have just opened is a template for your trading cards. You will design a card in the top left rectangular guide. All of your work will be done in this space.

Step 2 Move the mouse to the tool bar and select the *text* tool. Drag a text frame that leaves a .25 inch (.6 cm) margin at the sides and bottom of the rectangular guide. Begin the text frame about 1/3 of the way down the card.

Step 3 Click on the **Center Align** button from the text ruler. Type in your name.

Step 4 Press the return or enter key to move the cursor down to the next line. Click on the **Left Align** button.

Step 5 Decide what information you want to include in your biography. The format of the card (paragraph, outline, bullets) is your choice. Type the information beneath your name.

Step 6 Highlight your name by moving the pointer arrow to it and clicking the mouse button three times. Do a text makeover on the words, making them no larger than 14 points.

Step 7 Move the mouse to the tool bar and click on the *Pointer Arrow*.

Step 8 Pull down the **FILE** menu and select ***Insert***.

Remember to choose the pointer arrow before inserting a graphic. If you do not, the picture will come into the document as a piece of text. You will not be able to resize or move it to another position.

Step 9 Follow the dialog boxes until you have located the file that contains your picture. Select it and then click on the **Insert** button.

Step 10 Use the corner grabber handles to resize the graphic. Drag any corner diagonally inward to make the picture smaller.

Step 11 Place the pointer arrow in the center of the picture and drag it to the empty space at the top of the card.

Step 12 Click on the *rectangle* tool from the tool bar. Draw a rectangle around the outer edge of the card.

Step 13 Click on the **Fill Pattern** palette in the tool bar and select a transparent fill. It is the one that shows two interlocking, clear boxes.

Step 14 Adjust the pen width, color, and pattern from the appropriate **Pen** palettes.

Your card cannot go beyond the gray card outline. If you need more room, try using a smaller font size or type (do not go smaller than 9 points). Making your picture smaller will give you more room for your text.

Career Trading Cards *(cont.)*

Step 15 Proofread and check the spelling of all of your work. When you are content with the way that your card looks, you are ready to copy it to the remaining eight rectangular guides.

Step 16 Pull down the **EDIT** menu and choose ***Select All***. Everything on the page is now selected, including the gray rectangular card guides.

Step 17 To deselect the card guides, choose the *pointer* tool from the tool bar. Hold down the shift key as you click the mouse button on the gray guide outline. You will know that they have been deselected when you no longer see the corner grabber boxes.

Step 18 Pull down the **EDIT** menu and choose ***Copy***.

Step 19 Move the mouse so that the pointer arrow is in the second rectangular guide. Click the mouse button. Pull down the **EDIT** menu and choose ***Paste***.

Step 20 Click on the pasted card and drag it so that it is properly placed within the gray guidelines of the second card.

Step 21 Repeat Steps 19 and 20 until each rectangular guide has a copy of your card.

Step 22 Use the side scroll arrow to move down to the second page of this document. You should see another set of gray rectangular guides. These are the places where you will be creating the flip side of your card.

Step 23 Leaving a .25 inch (.6 cm) margin at all edges of the top left rectangular guide, draw a text frame.

Step 24 Follow the same steps as you did for the biography card to create the flip side. This time, enter information about the career that you have chosen. When you are satisfied with the way that this side of the card looks, copy and paste it into the remaining eight rectangular guides.

Step 25 Pull down the **FILE** menu and select ***Save As***. Name the file (your name) *Trading Card.*

Step 26 Pull down the **FILE** menu and select ***Print***. Click on the **Print** button. Paste each page onto one side of a piece of cardstock paper. Carefully cut the page between the card frames. You now have nine copies of your personal Career Card. Begin collecting other cards by trading cards with your friends.

If your printer can hold heavy (cardstock) paper, you can print directly onto this paper. Begin by printing only page one. Take the printed piece of cardstock, turn it over, and print page two on the back side. Practice with plain paper first so that you know which end of the paper to place into the printer first.

If your school has a laminating machine, laminate each card. You have worked hard on this project, and your trading cards should last for a long time.

Career Trading Cards *(cont.)*

Teacher Task Card

Use these instructions to prepare a template that your students will use to create their own trading cards.

- Open a new *ClarisWorks* drawing program.
- Pull down the **FORMAT** menu and choose *Document*. Change the **Size** so that there are ***2 Pages Down***. Click on the **OK** button.
- Click on the *rectangle* tool from the tool bar. Draw a rectangle that is about 2 inches (5 cm) wide and 3 inches (8 cm) long.
- Change the pen color to gray.
- Pull down the **EDIT** menu and choose ***Copy***.
- Pull down the **EDIT** menu and choose ***Paste***.
- Repeat the paste process to make another copy of the first rectangle. Line the three guides across the top of the screen.
- Hold the shift key down as you click on all three boxes, selecting them.
- Pull down the **ARRANGE** menu and choose ***Align Objects***.
- Click in the circle next to *Align Top Edges*.
- With the three boxes still selected, pull down the **ARRANGE** menu and select ***Group***. These three items are now grouped together as one object.
- Copy and paste a second row of rectangular guides. After you have dragged this row to the correct position, paste another set below it.
- Shift-click on the three rows to select them all. Follow the above steps, this time aligning the objects on the left side.
- When the page is set up correctly, use **ARRANGE–*Group*** to group all nine guides as one object.
- Pull down the **EDIT** menu and ***Copy*** the guides.
- Use the scroll arrow to move down to page two of the document.
- Pull down the **EDIT** menu and choose ***Paste***. Adjust the placement of this second set of guides.
- Pull down the **FILE** menu and select ***Save As***. Click in the circle next to *Stationery*. Name the file *Trading Cards*. Click on the **Save** button.

Career Trading Cards *(cont.)*

Sample Template

Your Trading Card template is now ready to be used by your students. They will use the guide that you have created to design their own cards.

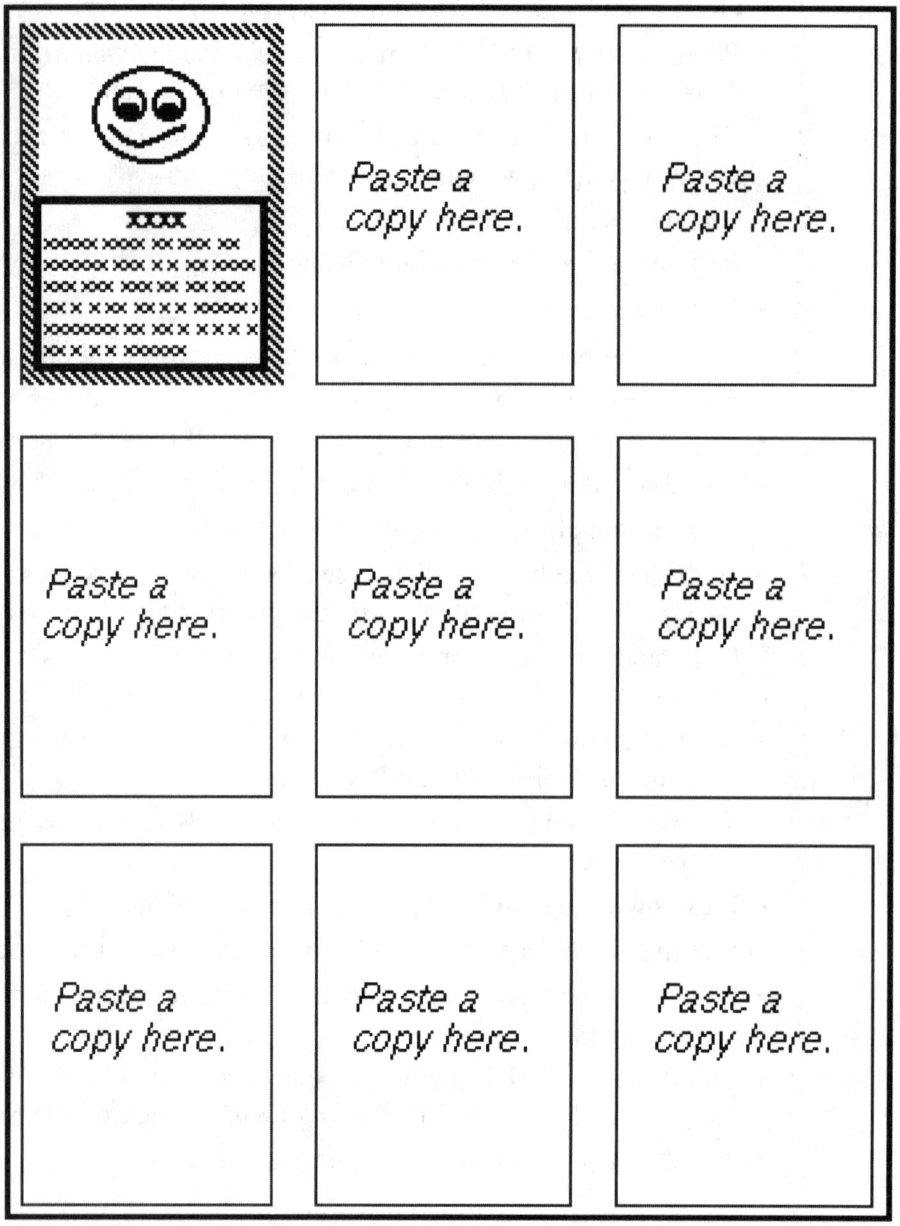

Using the Template

- Prepare your card in the rectangle guide at the top left corner of the screen.
- Select all of the objects in the card and copy them to the computer's clipboard.
- Paste a copy of the card into each of the remaining rectangular guides.

Career Trading Cards *(cont.)*

Work Sheet

Biographical Information
Planning Sheet

Name: ______________________________

Where were you born? ______________________________

Who are the people in your family?

____
____
____
____

What are some of the things that you like to do?

____
____
____
____

What special talents or hobbies do you have?

____
____
____
____

Tell about somewhere special that you have gone, or tell about something special that you have done.

____
____
____
____

Tell about your pet or somebody who is special to you.

____
____
____

Make enough copies of this work sheet so that each student can have his/her own planning page.

Career Trading Cards (cont.)

Work Sheet

Career Card

Research Planning Sheet

What career have you selected for this project?

____

Write a short description of what a person in this career does:

____

____

____

____

____

____

What special education or training will you need in order to work in this career?

____

____

____

Why would a person want to work in this profession?

____

____

____

How much money would you make if you worked in this field?

____

Where did you find your information?

____

Name ________________________ **Class** __________

Make enough copies of this work sheet so that each student can have his/her own

Career Trading Cards (cont.)

How to Create a Digitized Photograph

Before beginning this project you will need a digitized photograph of each student. There are several methods by which this task may be accomplished:

Use a QuickCam (Connectix)

This device looks like an eyeball that is sitting on the top of your computer. It can capture an image just like a camera would. A drawback to the QuickCam is that it must always be attached to the computer, thereby limiting the location of the pictures. The image is either placed on the computer's clipboard or saved to a disk. Appoint a camera crew who will take pictures of each student in the class. Each student should save the picture on his/her own floppy disk.

Use a Digital Camera

Many companies now produce digital cameras. They look and function just like regular cameras; however, they do not use film. Instead, the pictures are stored as digital images in the camera. You are not restricted as to where a picture can be taken. When you have finished taking your pictures, follow the directions in the camera's user manual to transfer the images from the camera to your computer. This device gives you flexibility regarding where you can take a photograph but adds additional steps before the images can be used in a document.

Use a Scanner

This device attaches directly to your computer. It operates in a similar manner to a photocopy machine. Instead of a paper copy coming out, a digital copy of the picture is saved in the computer's memory. Follow the directions that come with your scanner to save the digitized image in a format that can be inserted into another document.

Use Regular Film That Has Been Developed in Digital Format

Many film processors now offer this option when you have your film developed. No special equipment is necessary. Instead of receiving prints after your film has been processed, you receive a computer disk. The images on the disk can be inserted into your computer document.

Use Input from a Video tape

If your computer has a video-in port, you can capture images from a videotape. Connect your videotape player to your computer. Follow the directions in your user manual to select one frame from the video. Save it as a picture file that can be inserted into the computer document.

Go with the Flow

This Project

In this project your students will analyze problems and conflicts that characters in literature face and make predictions about their outcomes. A flow chart of these situations and resolutions will be constructed. Once each conflict has been identified, as a prereading assignment, students will predict what some possible solutions might be. After reading the book, the actual resolution to each problem will be noted on the flow chart.

Computer Skills

- drawing program
- using text frames
- text makeovers
- use of arrowheads

Before Beginning

- Discuss flow charts with your class. Students should be familiar with statement frames, decision frames, and directional arrows. Use the sample flow chart on page 48 to help your students identify these items.
- Use the sample flow chart on page 48 to practice using a flow chart. Model the use of a flow chart for a problem that a character in a book your class is reading is facing.

Quick Steps

- Open a new *ClarisWorks* drawing document.
- Draw a text frame in the middle of the top of the page. Select one of the problems that you have identified in your reading journal and enter it in the text frame.
- Draw a rectangle around the text frame.
- Before you continue to read the story, think of a few ways to solve this problem.
- Use a separate text frame to write each solution. Move the text frames so that they are in a horizontal line below the original problem.
- Draw a four-sided polygon around each solution.
- What might the consequences be for each of the solutions? Write them in separate text frames below each reaction.
- Draw an oval around each consequence.
- Draw a line with an arrowhead to show the way each problem, solution, and result flows.
- Save the file with the file name *Go with the Flow*.
- Continue to read the book. When you have identified the way the character actually solves his/her problems, note them in your literature journal. Were any of your predictions correct?
- Do a text makeover on the items in your flow chart that actually occur in the book.
- Save and print the file.

Go with the Flow *(cont.)*

Step 1 Open *ClarisWorks* and click on **Drawing**. Click on the **OK** button.

Step 2 Click on the *text* tool in the tool bar. Place the I-beam at the 2-inch (5 cm) marker on the ruler. Hold the mouse button down as you drag the I-beam across the top of the screen, stopping at the 6-inch (15 cm) marker. Choose one of the problems that you have identified in your reading journal and type it in the text frame.

Step 3 Click on the rectangle tool in the tool bar. Bring the crosshairs to the top left corner of the text frame. Hold the mouse button down as you drag the crosshairs across the text frame, drawing a rectangle around the words that you have typed.

If the rounded rectangle covers the words, choose a transparent fill pattern from the fill pattern palette. This is the pattern with two interlocking, clear boxes.

Do not read any more of the story. Try to think of some possible solutions to the problem. What can the character do?

Step 4 Click on the *text* tool on the tool bar. Draw a text frame that goes about 1/3 of the way across the page. Type in one of the possible solutions that you thought of.

Step 5 Repeat Step 4 to create a separate text frame for each of the possible solutions that you identified.

Step 6 Click on the *pointer arrow* on the tool bar. Use the pointer arrow to select one of the text frames. Hold the mouse button down as you drag the text frame until it is next to the text frame that you originally created in Step 4. Line up all of the solutions horizontally.

Step 7 If there are more solutions than will fit on one line, change the width of the text frames by dragging the corner handles in towards the center of the frame.

Step 8 Click on the *polygon* tool from the tool bar. Pull down the **OPTIONS** menu and select ***Polygon Sides***. Change the number of sides to four. Click on the **OK** button.

Step 9 Place the crosshairs above the center of the text of the first solution. While holding down the mouse button, drag the mouse to the right and down. Continue until the shape that you are drawing is large enough to cover the text of the first solution. You can rotate the shape by moving the mouse around until the corners are pointed up, down, left, and right.

The size of the quadrangle, as well as the text field, can be adjusted so that they fit neatly on the screen. First, select the object with the pointer arrow and then make the text frame or quadrangle thinner, wider, taller, or shorter by dragging on one of the corner grabber handles. You decide how you want the solution box to look.

Step 10 Click the mouse button on the text tool on the tool bar. Bring the crosshairs back to the writing screen and make a text frame beneath the first solution box. Type in a possible consequence for that action.

Go with the Flow *(cont.)*

Step 11 Create a separate text frame below each solution and write what the results of that action might be.

Step 12 Click on the *oval* tool on the tool bar. Bring the crosshairs above the first consequence box and drag the mouse to the right and down, drawing an oval around the words. Adjust the oval to fit around the words.

Step 13 Draw an oval around each consequence box. Be certain that the fill pattern for these ovals is transparent.

Step 14 Click on the *Arrows* palette on the tool bar and choose ***Arrow At End***.

Step 15 Click on the *straight line* tool on the tool bar. Draw lines that connect the statement frame with each of the possible solutions.

Step 16 Draw a line that connects each solution with its appropriate consequence. Remember to use the arrow to indicate the correct flow of events.

Step 17 Pull down the **FILE** menu and select ***Save As***. Name the file *Go with the Flow* and click on the **Save** button.

Continue to read the book. What does the character do to resolve the problem that he/she has? Write what actually happens in your literature journal. Did you make any correct predictions?

Step 18 Open *ClarisWorks* and click on the **Cancel** button. Pull down the **FILE** menu and select ***Open***.

Step 19 Find the file called *Go with the Flow* and click the mouse button on it. Click on the **Open** button.

Step 20 Locate any solutions and/or consequences in your flow chart that actually happened in the book. Do a font makeover for these items.

Step 21 Click on the pointer arrow in the tool bar. Click on the shape that you drew around the correct decision and result to select each one. Use the *pen width* palette to change the size of the line in these shapes. Make it 6 points.

Step 22 Pull down the **FILE** menu and select ***Save As***. Click on the **Save** button. Yes, you do want to replace the existing file.

Step 23 Pull down the **FILE** menu and select ***Print***. Click on the **Print** button to print a copy of your flow chart.

Go with the Flow (cont.)

Practice Flow Chart

C.J. loves to listen to music. The first thing he does whenever he goes to his room to do his homework is turn on his stereo. With the music playing, C.J. often finds that it is difficult to concentrate on his schoolwork, but C.J. loves his music. It was the night before a big history test, and C.J. knew that he really needed to study.

This flow chart shows what might happen to C.J. Which box is the statement frame? What are the decisions that C.J. might make? Which boxes show the consequences of each decision?

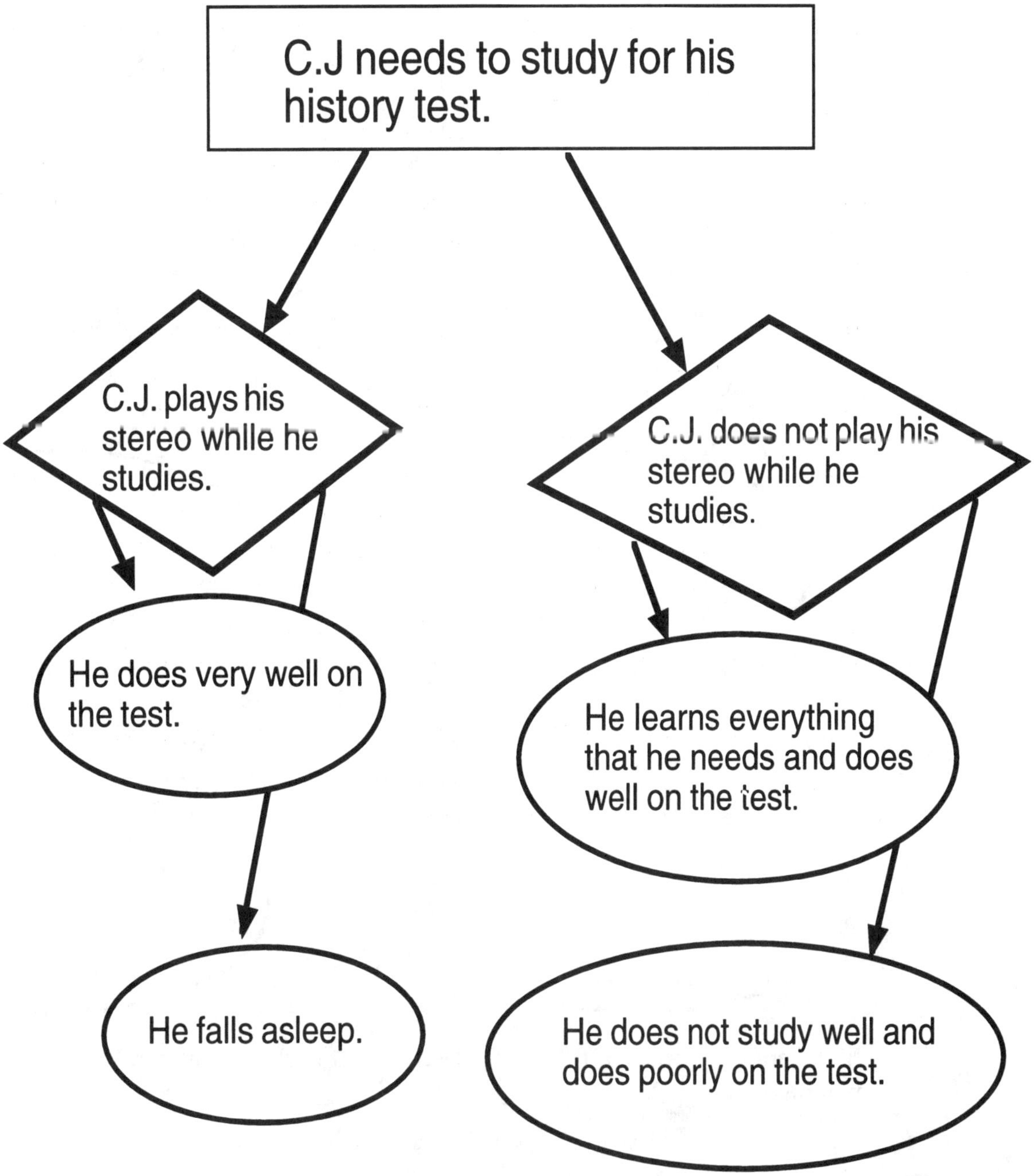

Go with the Flow (cont.)

Student Work Sheet

Use this sample flow chart to diagram how a character in a book that your class has read might solve a problem that he/she faces.

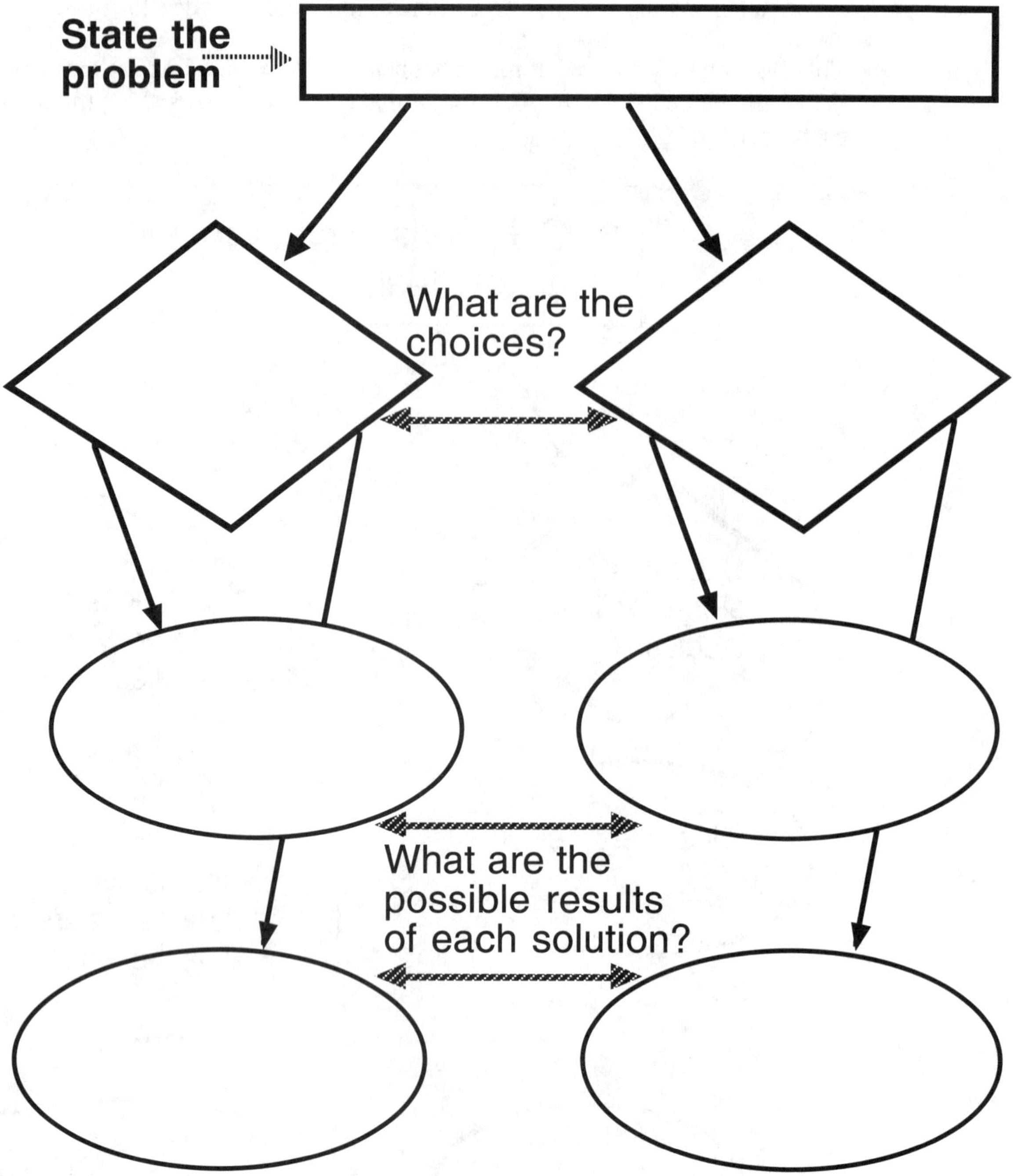

Make enough copies of this work sheet so that each student can have his/her own planning page.

In the Beginning

This Project

In this project your students will demonstrate how well they understand the plot and sequence of a book or story that they have read. Valuable study skills are used as students form an outline of the main events of a story. These topics are jumbled, challenging other students to place them in the correct sequence.

Computer Skills

- drawing
- manipulating text frames
- text makeovers

Before Beginning

- Use the sample story on page 52 to practice making an outline. Which items would be considered the main points of this story?
- Select a passage from literature that your students are familiar with. As a class, identify a few of the main ideas. Use the Student Work Sheet on page 53 to model how an outline is formed with the main ideas. Fill in the supporting information.
- Group students in pairs, and instruct them to use the planning page to form an outline for this project, using a book or story that they have read.

Quick Steps

- Open a new *ClarisWorks* drawing document.
- Write the name of the book or story that you are using in a text frame at the top of the page.
- Create a separate text frame for each item in a *What Happened?* box on the planning page outline.
- Do a text makeover for these topic headings, making the size 14 points and adjusting the way that the words look.
- Move the text frames so that they are not in the correct order.
- Save the file with the file name *In the Beginning*.
- Challenge another pair of students to place the story's events in the correct order. The second group of students needs to open the file called *In the Beginning*.
- Move the text frames so that they are read in the proper sequence.
- Fill in details that explain each event, using a normal font, size, and style.
- Save and print the completed work.
- Compare the information that is presented and its sequence with the data on the original planning sheet. Does the work demonstrate that the students know what happened in *In the Beginning?*

In the Beginning *(cont.)*

Step 1 Open a new *ClarisWorks* document. Click on **Drawing** and then click on **OK**.

Step 2 Click on the *text* tool in the tool bar. Hold the mouse button down as you drag the mouse across the top of the screen. Type the name of the book or story that you are using into this text frame.

You could also use a word processing document to create this project, but a drawing document allows easier movement of text frames. If you would prefer to use a word processing document, you will still need to create separate text frames for each item. After selecting the text tool, hold down the option key as you drag a text frame. This object can be selected and moved just like one that has been created in a drawing program.

Step 3 Click on the *text* tool in the tool bar. Hold down the mouse button as you drag the mouse across the screen, creating a text frame. Use the planning page that you prepared to write the first item from a *What Happened?* box.

Step 4 Repeat Step 3 to make a separate text frame in which you will write each theme that is in a *What Happened?* box.

Step 5 Do a text makeover on all of these topic headings. Pull down the **FONT** menu and choose the font that you will use. Pull down the **SIZE** menu and select ***14 point***. Pull down the **STYLE** menu and select the way that you want these words to look. Use the same makeover criteria for all of the text frames.

Remember to select (highlight) the text before you attempt to change the way that it looks. Otherwise, nothing will be adjusted.

Step 6 Click on the *pointer arrow* in the tool bar. Click on a text frame to select it. You know the object has been selected when you see the four small grabber handles (squares) in the corners of the frame. Drag the text frame so that it is in another position.

Step 7 Repeat Step 6 until all of the text frames have been moved and are not in the correct order.

Step 8 Pull down the **FILE** menu and select ***Save As***. Give the file the name *In the Beginning*. Click on the **Save** button to save your work.

In the Beginning *(cont.)*

Challenge another pair of students to place your story's events into the correct order while you try to rearrange the story outline that they have created.

Step 9 Once the *ClarisWorks* program has been opened, pull down the **FILE** menu and select ***Open***. Locate the correct file name and click on it. Click on the **Open** button.

Step 10 Click on the *pointer arrow* from the tool bar. Use this tool to select the text frame that tells what happened in the beginning of the story. Hold the mouse button down as you drag the text frame to the top of the screen.

Step 11 Select each of the remaining text frames and reposition them so that they can be read in the proper sequence.

Step 12 Click on the *text* tool in the tool bar. Bring the mouse to the first text frame. Click the mouse button to place the I-beam after the main idea that is already there.

Step 13 Press return or enter to move the cursor to the next line.

Step 14 Pull down the **SIZE** menu and choose ***12 point***.

Step 15 Pull down the **STYLE** menu and choose ***Plain text*** to return to the usual way that words appear.

Step 16 Fill in supporting information that explains what happened during this occurrence. Write a short paragraph about each event.

Step 17 Repeat Steps 12–16 for each of the text frames.

Step 18 Pull down the **FILE** menu and select ***Save As***. Give the file the name *It all began . . ..* Click on the **Save** button to save your work.

Step 19 Pull down the **FILE** menu and choose ***Print***. Click on the print button.

Step 20 Meet with the people who created the original *In the Beginning* file. Compare the information that you have added to the outline and the order in which you have placed it with the details that were on the original planning sheet. Do your ideas match? Do both teams agree about what happened *In the Beginning*?

In the Beginning *(cont.)*

Read this story with your class. Use the outline form to place the events that happened into their proper sequence. After you have identified the main ideas, list any additional information that pertains to that event.

Once upon a time there was a young lady named Matilda. She was quite beautiful, but somehow felt that her life was unfulfilled. She thought that there had to be more to experience than her daily routines. She lived with her stepmother and three evil stepsisters. They thought that Matilda was there to answer their every need. "Wash the floor, scrub the windows, darn my socks," was all that Matilda heard each day. There just had to be more to life.

On one particularly dreary day, a letter arrived from the king. He was planning a grand ball. Matilda was thrilled. At last she would have an opportunity to get out and party. Alas, this was not what her sisters had in mind. They refused to help Matilda prepare for the ball.

Matilda needed a plan. She ran down to the mall and bought the necessary supplies. She would design and make her own gown. She called on her friends to assist her in getting ready. Her hair, nails, and accessories needed to be perfect. She would be the queen of the ball.

What Happened?

- ***Supporting Information***
- ***Supporting Information***
- ***Supporting Information***

What Happened?

- ***Supporting Information***
- ***Supporting Information***
- ***Supporting Information***

What Happened?

- ***Supporting Information***
- ***Supporting Information***
- ***Supporting Information***

Make enough copies of this work sheet so that each student can have his/her own planning page.

In the Beginning (cont.)

Student Work Sheet

As a class, select a passage from a book you have read. Identify some of the main ideas and occurrences that influence each event. Use this work sheet to create an outline of what happened in the book.

What Happened?

- **Supporting Information**
- **Supporting Information**
- **Supporting Information**

What Happened?

- **Supporting Information**
- **Supporting Information**
- **Supporting Information**

What Happened?

- **Supporting Information**
- **Supporting Information**
- **Supporting Information**

Let's Talk About It

This Project

In this project your students will transform a narrative into a dialog. After reading a short story or essay, they will identify the principal characters, decide what role each person played in the story, and write the script for a dialog that might have occurred.

Computer Skills

- word processing
- indent markers
- text makeovers

Before Beginning

- Use the work sheet on page 56 to practice identifying characters, theme, and point of view.
- Select pieces of literature that your students will use for this project. They might want to choose an excerpt from a book that they have read, or you might want to provide material that is appropriate to your classwork.
- Place your students into groups of three or four. The planning sheet on page 57 will help them organize their dialogs.

Quick Steps

- Open a new *ClarisWorks* word processing document.
- Write a brief description that sets the time and place of the story. Italicize the entire paragraph.
- Adjust the left margin so that it is at the 1.5-inch (3.84 cm) marker.
- Adjust the right margin so that it is at the 7-inch (18 cm) marker.
- Type in the name of the character who speaks first, followed by a colon (:).
- Enter the words that he/she will say.
- Begin the text for each new speaker on a new line. Start with his/her name, followed by a colon.
- Do a text makeover on the words that will be spoken. Create an individual text style for each speaker.
- Save the file with the file name *Let's Talk About It.*
- Print a copy of the dialog.
- Perform your play for your class.

Let's Talk About It *(cont.)*

Step 1 Open *ClarisWorks* and select **Word Processing**. Click on the **OK** button.

Step 2 Using the excerpt from literature that you have selected for this project, type in a short paragraph that sets the time and place of the story. Drag the mouse across the entire paragraph to select it.

A shortcut for selecting an entire paragraph is quadruple clicking. Try it now. Move the mouse to place the I-beam at any spot in the paragraph. Quickly click the mouse button four times. The whole paragraph is highlighted.

Step 3 Pull down the **STYLE** menu and choose ***Italic***. We will use this type style whenever you have written a description or instruction and not dialog.

Step 4 Move the mouse so that the pointer arrow is on the left margin marker. It probably is the number 1 on the ruler (that is the default value). Hold down the mouse button as you drag the margin marker to the 1.5-inch (3.84 cm) point on the ruler. The indent marker will move also. That's fine; we want it to go along.

Step 5 Drag the right margin marker to the 7-inch (18 cm) point on the ruler.

Step 6 Decide which character will be talking first. Type in his/her name and then type a colon (:).

Step 7 Write the words that this person will be saying.

Step 8 When you are ready to have the next person speak, press return or enter to bring the cursor to a new line. Repeat Steps 6 and 7 for each new piece of dialog.

Step 9 Locate the first section of dialog. Hold down the mouse button as you highlight that text. Do a text makeover on the selected text.

Step 10 Find all of the portions of the dialog that the character in Step 9 speaks. Use the same text styles as you did in Step 9 to make over all of his/her words.

Step 11 Identify the remaining characters in the dialog, and do text makeovers for their words, following Steps 9 and 10. Give each person a text font and style that is unique.

Step 12 Pull down the **FILE** menu and select ***Save As***. Give the file the file name *Let's Talk About It*. Click on the **Save** button.

Step 13 Pull down the **FILE** menu and select ***Print***. Set the number of copies to the number of characters that there are. Click on the **Print** button.

Step 14 Use your scripts as you orally present your play to your class.

Let's Talk About It *(cont.)*

Work Sheet

To the teacher: Before beginning this work sheet, your class will need to read the story about Matilda that is found on page 52 of this book. If you have already completed *In the Beginning*, they will have the story from the work sheet. If not, copy the story onto a transparency and display it with an overhead projector, or print copies of the story for them to use.

Use this work sheet to help you identify characters, theme, and point of view. Read the story about Matilda, woman of the 90s. Fill in the story map with information that you have gathered.

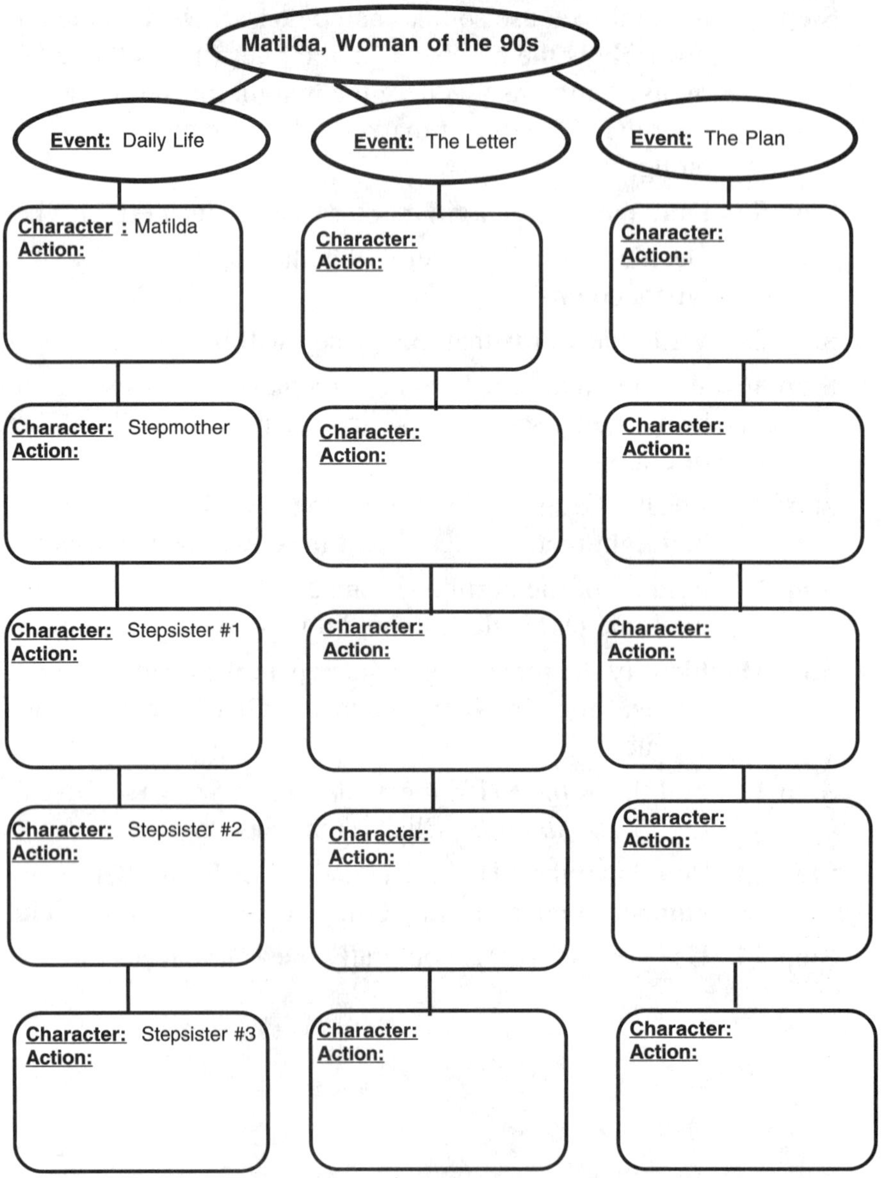

Make enough copies of this work sheet so that each student can have his/her own planning page.

Let's Talk About It *(cont.)*

Planning Page

Use this planning page to help you prepare to write your dialog. List a few events from the story that you are using. How did each character react to that event?

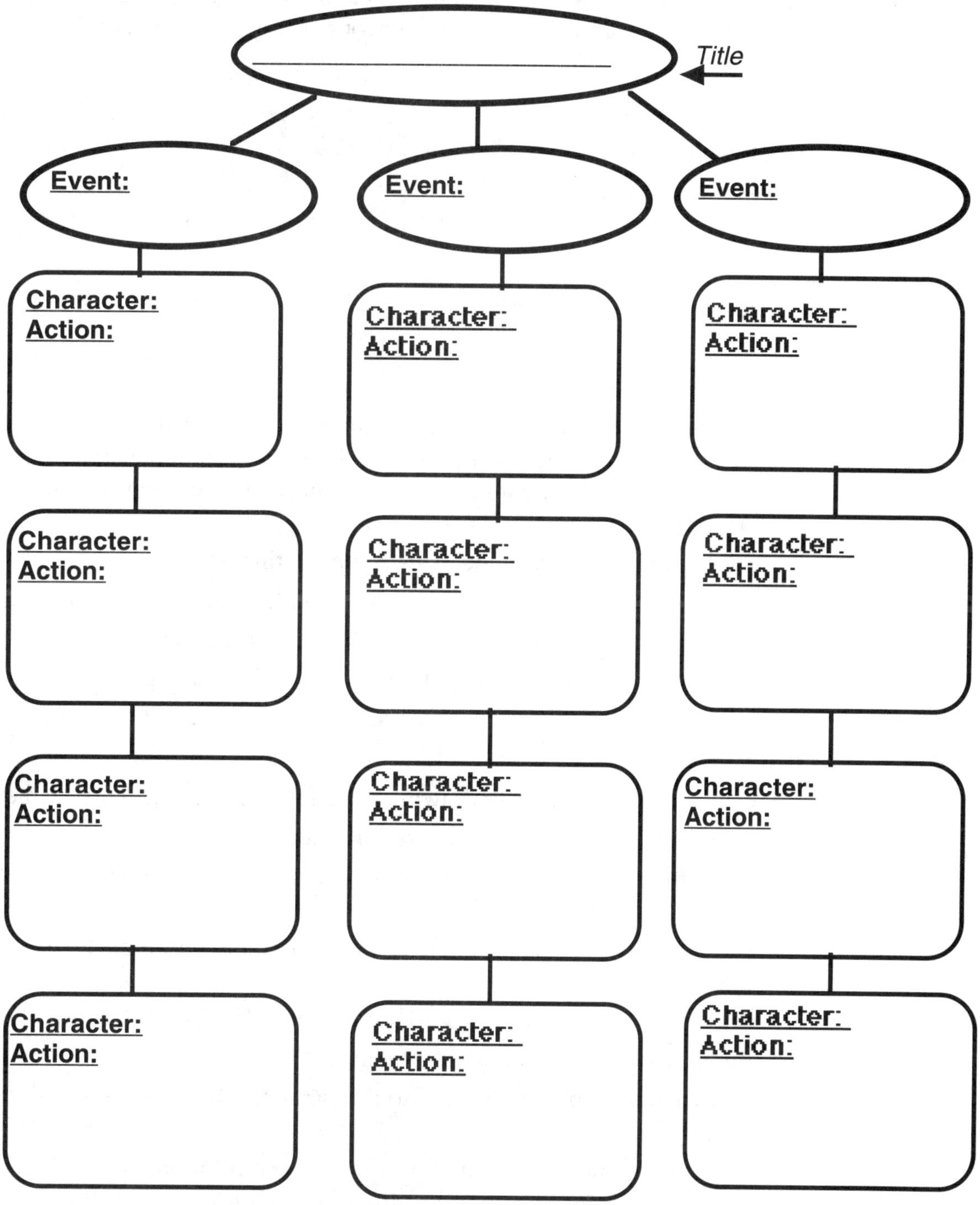

Make enough copies of this work sheet so that each student can have his/her own planning sheet.

A New World

This Project

Your students will chart unexplored areas in this project. When they take an imaginary journey into space, they will discover a planet that has never before been seen. Their task is to record important data about this planet. Using information from sources that already exist, they must form conclusions about their new planet. Their task in this project is to create a travel poster that encourages people to visit this new planet.

Computer Skills

- drawing program
- painting program
- text frames
- inserting graphics
- manipulating text frames

Before Beginning

- Students need a background knowledge of our solar system. They should understand the relationship of proximity to the sun and temperature, the time needed for one revolution, and the size of the planets and their position in the galaxy.
- Form groups of three students to complete this project.
- Complete the work sheet on page 61 as a planning guide for the travel posters.
- Decide what information will be included on each poster.
- Gather pictures that you might want to include on the poster.

Quick Steps

- Open a new *ClarisWorks* drawing document. Save it with the name of your planet.
- Open a new *ClarisWorks* painting program
- Write the name of the new planet in a text frame. Do a text makeover, making it at least 72 points.
- Select the planet's name and use one of the transform tools to change the way it looks.
- Copy the selected text object to the computer's clipboard.
- Return to the original drawing document.
- Paste the name of the planet onto this screen. Move it to a prominent position on the page.
- Create a separate text frame for each piece of information.
- Use free rotate to change the angle of the text frame.
- Insert some of the graphics that you have located, positioning them where you want them.

A New World *(cont.)*

Step 1 Open *ClarisWorks* and select a **Drawing** document. Click on the **OK** button.

Step 2 Pull down the **EDIT** menu and select ***Save As***. Name the file with the name of the planet you have discovered. Click on the **Save** button.

Step 3 Pull down the **FILE** menu and choose ***New*** to begin another document. Choose a ***Painting*** document this time. This will be your work sheet on which you will create fancy headings to use in your poster.

Step 4 In the painting document, click on the *text* tool. Hold down the mouse button as you drag it across the page, forming a text frame. Type the name of your planet in the text frame.

Step 5 Drag the mouse over the text to highlight it. Do a text makeover, changing the size of the letters to be at least 72 points. Make any other changes that you want.

Step 6 Choose the *selection rectangle* tool from the tool bar. Place the crosshairs at the top left corner of the name of the planet. Hold the mouse button down as you drag the mouse across the text, forming a selecting frame around the word. This frame is a broken line that seems to be moving.

When you are working in a painting document, it is necessary to identify the part of the picture with which you want to work. Since there are no separate objects (as there are in a drawing document) you must select a section before manipulating or changing it. When you click anywhere else on the screen or choose another tool, the area becomes deselected. Be careful.

Step 7 Pull down the **TRANSFORM** menu and select ***Perspective***. Notice how the selection frame has small, open boxes in each corner. These grabber handles allow you to change the way the items in a selection frame appear. Experiment for a while. What happens when you pull the top left corner to the left? How is the shape changed when you drag the bottom right corner down? Find a look that you like.

Step 8 With the text still selected, pull down the **EDIT** menu. Choose ***Copy*** to place the item on the computer's clipboard. If the item has become deselected (it does not have the moving frame around it), choose the *selection rectangle* from the tool bar and drag a frame around it again.

Step 9 Pull down the **VIEW** menu and select the name of your planet from the bottom of the list. You are now back to the drawing document that you will use to create your travel poster.

Step 10 Click on the *pointer arrow* tool on the tool bar. Pull down the **FILE** menu and choose ***Paste***. The name of the planet is now on the screen as a graphic object.

Step 11 Select the planet's name by clicking the pointer arrow on it. The selected object will have four black grabber handles in the corners. Drag the frame to the place on the screen that you think looks the best.

A New World *(cont.)*

Step 12 Click on the *text* tool on the tool bar. Drag the mouse across the screen for about 3 inches (8 cm), creating a text frame. Type a short blurb about one of the pieces of information that you want to include on your poster.

Step 13 Choose the *pointer arrow* from the tool bar and click it on the text frame. Hold down the mouse button as you drag the text frame to where you want it to be on the page.

Step 14 Pull down the **TRANSFORM** menu and choose ***Free Rotate***. Place the small x at one of the corner gabber handles. Hold down the mouse button as you drag the mouse in a small circle. Notice how the entire text frame rotates with you. Your words do not have to stay in horizontal lines anymore. Using Free Rotate allows you to change the angle of the text frame.

Step 15 When the text is the way you want it to be, you need to turn the free rotate function off. Pull down the **TRANSFORM** menu. The Free Rotate selection has a check next to it. That shows that it is currently in use. Click on ***Free Rotate***, and the check is gone. This choice is no longer in use.

Step 16 Repeat Steps 11 to 14 for each item of information that you want to place on your poster.

Step 17 Pull down the **FILE** menu and select ***Library***. Find a category of graphics that will look good on your poster. Select the picture and drag it to the main screen. Click in the close box of the graphics library to take it off of the screen.

Step 18 You are not limited to the items that are in the *ClarisWorks* library. Use some of the techniques from page 9 (How to Add a Picture) to place some interesting artwork in your poster.

Step 19 Drag the graphics to the places where they look the best.

Step 20 Pull down the **FILE** menu and select ***Save As***. Keep the same file name, and click on the **Save** button. Yes, you do want to replace the old file with this new one.

Step 21 Pull down the **FILE** menu and select ***Print***. Click on the **Print** button to make a hard copy of your work.

Step 22 Make an oral presentation to your class, explaining why a person might want to travel to your new planet. Explain what they would find there. Use the poster and other materials (from Related Activities) to support your presentation.

A New World *(cont.)*

Student Work Sheet

Names ______________________________
Class ________

Congratulations! You have just discovered a new planet. Create a poster that tells about the new planet. Use this planning sheet to gather important data about your planet.

Name of Planet ______________________________

Nearest known planet __________________________________

Distance from earth ____________________

What does the planet look and feel like? ___________________

What is the temperature? ________________

Describe the atmosphere? What elements are found here?

____

____

Is there life on this planet? ____________

What are the life forms like? _____________________________

____

____

____

If there is <u>no</u> life, why not? _____________________________

____

____

What would an earth visitor need in order to survive here?

____

____

Make enough copies of this work sheet so that each student can have his/her own planning page.

Weather or Not

This Project

Your students will analyze data that they have gathered as they predict weather trends. After they have recorded weather reports from four different cities on a spreadsheet, they will graph the information and compare weather systems. This project allows your students to see the similarities and differences in the weather in cities that are in longitudes and latitudes similar to their own.

Computer Skills

- spreadsheet
- entering data
- graphs

Before Beginning

- Students should be familiar with various components of a weather report. You might want to include high temperature, low temperature, precipitation, wind velocity, barometric pressure, and relative humidity.
- Divide the class into groups of two for this project. Choose one weather component that each group will include in its spreadsheet.
- Select a city that is in a similar longitude to your own. Locate a city that has a similar latitude to yours. Find a city that has a similar longitude to your latitude buddy city. These are the cities for which you will be recording the weather. Information can be found in local newspapers, through the weather channel on television, or on the Internet (www.weather.com).
- Use the work sheet on page 66 to record the information that you will need for this project.
- Use the Teacher Task Card on page 65 to create a template for this project.

Quick Steps

- Open the *ClarisWorks* file called *Weather*.
- Type a title for your spreadsheet into cell A1.
- Enter the names of the four cities that you will be using in column A, beginning in cell A5.
- Beginning in cell B3, enter the dates for which you will be recording data in the cells in row 3.
- Record the appropriate information for each city and date in the correct cell.
- Select all cells from A5 through F8.
- Make a bar graph of the information.
- Save the file with the file name (type of weather recorded [for example, High Temperature]).
- Print your spreadsheet and graph.

Weather or Not *(cont.)*

Step 1 Open *ClarisWorks*, and click on the **Cancel** button.

Step 2 Pull down the **FILE** menu and select ***Open***. Find the file called *Weather* and click the *pointer arrow* on it. Click on the **Open** button.

Step 3 Move the mouse until you are pointing to cell A1. Click the mouse to make this cell the active one. Retype a title for your spreadsheet. If you are tracking the high temperatures for your cities, you might want to enter "Weather Report—High Temperature." Press return or enter to move your information from the entry bar to the active cell.

Step 4 Click the mouse in cell A5 to make it the active cell. Replace the current words with the name of your home city in the entry bar. Press return or enter to move the information from the entry bar to the active cell.

Step 5 Cell A6 is the new active cell. By default, the next active cell is the one directly beneath the previous entry. Type the name of another city in this cell. Press return or enter to place the information in the cell.

Step 6 Repeat Step 5 until column A contains the names of the four cities that you have selected.

Step 7 Move the mouse until you are pointing to cell B3. Click the mouse button to make this the active cell. Replace the word "date" with the first date for which you will be recording information. Press return or enter to move the information from the entry bar to the active cell.

Step 8 Click the mouse in cell C3 to make it the active cell. Type the next date for which you will be recording information. Press return or enter to move the information from the entry bar to the active cell.

Step 9 Repeat Step 9 until row 3 contains all of the dates for which you will be recording information.

Step 10 Enter the information that you have gathered on your work sheet into the correct cells.

Remember to click the mouse on a cell to select it and make it the active cell. Also remember to press return or enter to move the information from the entry bar to the selected cell.

	A	B	C	D	E
1	High Temperature				
2					
3		10/6	10/7	10/8	10/9
4					
5	Raleigh/Durham	88	87	84	84.00
6	New York	85	84	73	78.00
7	Portland	56	57	62	58.00
8	Los Angeles	67	86	77	81.00
9					

Weather or Not *(cont.)*

Step 11 Move the pointer arrow to cell A5. Hold down the mouse button as you drag the move to cell F8. This will select all of the cells in the spreadsheet.

Step 12 Pull down the **OPTIONS** menu and choose ***Make Chart***. We are going to use the information that you have selected to draw a graph.

Step 13 Click on the **Bar** button to create a bar graph. You can also make other types of graphs to display your information, but for now, we are going to make a bar graph.

Step 14 Click on the **Axes** button. Click in the circle next to the Y-axis and label it *High Temperature* (or the name of the weather condition that you are charting).

Step 15 Click in the circle next to the X-axis and label it *Days*. You can also change the minimum and maximum readings if you want a narrower range on your graph. Click on the **OK** button to return to the main chart options dialog box.

Step 16 Click on the **Labels** button. Type in a title for this graph. Click in one of the little circles to select where you want the title to be placed and how you want it to look.

Step 17 Adjust the way you want the legend box to appear by clicking in the appropriate boxes. Click on the **OK** button to return to the main chart options dialog box.

Step 18 When you have selected all of the chart options that you want to use, click on the **OK** button. The graph that is on your screen is an object. You can drag it and resize it until it is placed where you want it to be.

If you want to make any changes to the graph, just double-click on it. This returns you to the chart options dialog box. Make your changes and then click on the **OK** button.

Step 19 Pull down the **FILE** menu and select ***Save As***. Give the file the name of the type of weather variable that you have been charting (for example, *High Temperature*). Click on the **Save** button.

Step 20 Pull down the **FILE** menu and select ***Print***. Click on the **Print** button to print your spreadsheet and graph.

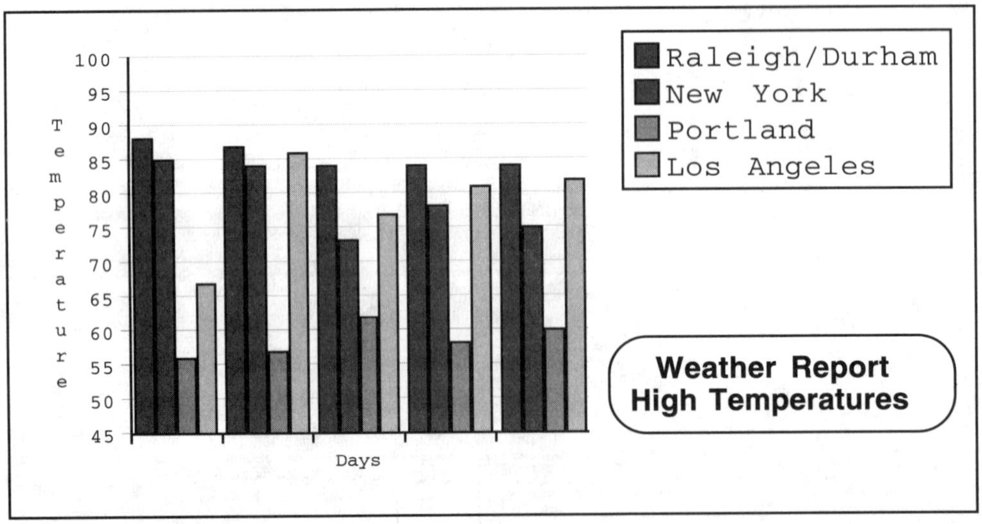

Weather or Not *(cont.)*

Teacher Task Card

Follow these directions to create a template for the spreadsheets that your students will be using to enter the information in their weather reports.

Step 1 Open a new *ClarisWorks* spreadsheet document.

Step 2 Click the mouse in cell A1 to make it the active cell. Type in the words *Weather Report*. Press return or enter to move the information from the entry bar to the active cell.

Step 3 Click in cell A5 to make it the active cell. Type in the words *City #1*. Press the return or enter key to move the information from the entry bar to the active cell.

Step 4 Repeat Step 3 for cities 2, 3, and 4.

Step 5 Click in cell B3 to make it the active cell. Type in the words *Date*. Press the return or enter key to move the information from the entry bar to the active cell.

Step 6 Repeat Step 5 for cells C3, D3 and E3.

Step 7 Pull down the **EDIT** menu and choose ***Select All.***

Step 8 Pull down the **FORMAT** menu and choose ***Size***. Select ***14 point***.

Step 9 Pull down the **FORMAT** menu and choose ***Style***. Select ***Bold***.

Step 10 Adjust the size of each row and column so that all of the words can be seen.

Step 11 Pull down the **FILE** menu and select ***Save As***. Name the file *Weather*. Click in the small circle next to the word "Stationery." Click on the **Save** button. This will save your work as a template for your students to use.

Sample Teacher Template

	A	B	C	D	E
1	Weather Report * * * * * * * * * * *				
2					
3		Date	Date	Date	Date
4					
5	City #1				
6	City #2				
7	City #3				
8	City #4				
9					

Weather or Not *(cont.)*

Work Sheet

Use this work sheet to organize the information that you are gathering for this project. Remember to record your information on the correct day and enter the data in the correct box. Always cite the source of your information.

Names of Weather Watchers ______________________________

Weather Condition being monitored ______________________________

Cities included in this report ______________________________

____

	City	City	City	City
Date				
Date				
Date				
Date				
Date				
Date				
Date				
Date				
Date				
Date				
Date				
Date				
Date				
Date				
Date				

Key to Sources:

WWW	World Wide Web	______________	(URL)
News	Newspaper	______________	(Name)
TV	Television	______________	(Station)
Rad	Radio	______________	(Station)

sample

85°	WWW

Make enough copies of this work sheet so that each group can have its own planning page.

How Loud Is Loud?

This Project

In this project your students will work on identifying the intensity of sound. They will look (and listen) around their own environments and classify the intensity of the different sounds that they hear. They will be asked to make judgments regarding the sounds that they hear every day.

Computer Skills

- database
- entering data
- sorting data

Before Beginning

- Students should be familiar with the concept of intensity of sound. They should know that the amount of energy that is carried by a sound wave over a period of time is called the intensity. The loudness of a sound is determined by its intensity.
- Discuss how sound intensity is measured. Students should be familiar with the unit for measuring sound, the decibel (dB).
- The work sheet on page 70 contains the sound levels for some familiar noises. Fill in the sound category (soft, average, and loud) for each item.
- Use a tape recorder to record various sounds. Have your students try to identify what is making each sound. Classify the sounds as soft, average, and loud.
- Have your students be sound detectives and record some sounds that they find around the school and neighborhood.
- Use the work sheet on page 70 to record your students' impressions of the sounds that they find around the school and neighborhood. In what intensity category would each sound be placed?

Quick Steps

- Open a new *ClarisWorks* database document.
- Create the following fields: Sound, Decibels, Category.
- Use the sound levels that are listed on the work sheet on page 70 to enter information into your database.
- Sort the information by intensity.
- Create a new record for each sound that was identified on the work sheet and enter the information for it.
- Sort the information by intensity category.
- Save your file with the file name *How Loud?*
- Use a list format to print a copy of the sounds in your database. Use this information to complete the work sheet on page 70.

How Loud Is Loud? *(cont.)*

Step 1 Open *ClarisWorks* and click the mouse on **Database**. Click on the **OK** button.

Step 2 Type the word *Sound* in the field name box. The blinking cursor lets you know that the computer is waiting for you to enter information into this box. Click on the **Create** button.

Step 3 Type the word *Decibels* in the field name box.

Whenever an item is highlighted (has a colored bar on top of it) anything that you type will replace the current words. When you are defining database fields, you do not have to delete the first field name before typing the second one.

Step 4 Move the mouse until the pointer is on the box next to field type. The triangle tells you that there is a menu of items that can be pulled down. Hold down the mouse button and select ***Number***. Click on the **Create** button.

Step 5 Type the word *Category* in the field name box. Click on the **Create** button.

Step 6 Click on the **Done** button.

Step 7 Pull down the **LAYOUT** menu and select ***List***.

Step 8 Move the pointer arrow to the top of the screen and point to the line separating the first two columns. Notice how the arrow becomes a double arrow. Hold down the mouse button and drag it to the right, changing the size of the first column. Make this column about 2 inches (5 cm) wide.

Step 9 Adjust the width of each column so that all of the headings show.

Step 10 This is a good time to save your work. Pull down the **FILE** menu and select ***Save As***. Name your file *How Loud?* Click on the **Save** button.

Step 11 Move the mouse until the arrow is pointing to the first box under the word **Sound**. Click the mouse button to place the cursor in that box. Use the work sheet on page 70 to enter the name of the first sound (Quiet Classroom).

Step 12 Press the tab key to move to the next field. Enter the decibel reading for a quiet classroom (35 dB).

Step 13 Press the tab key to move to the next field and enter the category this sound should be placed in.

How Loud Is Loud? *(cont.)*

Step 14 Pull down the **EDIT** menu and select ***New Record***.

Step 15 Repeat Steps 11 to 14 to transfer all of the information from the top part of your work sheet to your database.

Save your work from time to time, or you might be sorry later. You never know when the power to your computer will accidentally be turned off.

Step 16 Pull down the **ORGANIZE** menu and choose ***Sort Records***.

Step 17 From the field list box, click on the ***Decibels*** field. Click on the **Move** button.

This is telling the computer that you want to sort this list by decibels. Click on the **OK** button. The softest sound is now at the top of your list, and the loudest sound is at the bottom.

Step 18 Create a new record and enter the information for each of the sounds that you identified on the worksheet. You will need to begin with Step 14 and then follow Steps 11 to 14.

Step 19 Pull down the **ORGANIZE** menu and choose ***Sort Records***.

Step 20 From the field list box, click on the ***Category*** field. Click on the **Move** button.

This is telling the computer that you want to sort this list by category. Click on the **OK** button. All of the sounds are now grouped by categories. Notice that within each category, the items are listed in ascending order of loudness. Why do you think this happened?

Step 21 Pull down the **FILE** menu and choose ***Save As***. Click on the **Save** button. Yes, you do want to replace the existing file.

Step 22 Pull down the **FILE** menu and choose ***Print***. Click on the **Print** button. Use this hard copy of your database to answer the questions on the bottom of your work sheet.

How Loud Is Loud? *(cont.)*

Work Sheet

Here are some sounds that you hear every day. How would you classify each one? Fill in the Category column with the words soft, average, or loud.

Sound	Decibels	Sound Category
Quiet classroom	35	
Conversation	65	
Loud music	95	
Rocket engine	200	
Thresholdofpain	120	
Fallenleaves	10	
Whisper	15	
Average home	45	
Rock concert	120	
Busystreettraffic	75	
Threshold of human hearing	0	
Very soft music	30	
Jet engine	170	
Conversation	65	
Vacuum cleaner	80	
Thunder		

Use this chart to record information about some of the sounds that you hear around your school and neighborhood. What do you estimate the decibel level is for these sounds?

Sound	Estimated Decibels	Sound Category

Into which sound category would each noise fall?

Use your database to help you answer these questions.

1. Which sounds will cause you pain? ____________________
2. Which sounds will be hard to hear in a noisy room? ____________________
3. What is the loudest sound on the chart? ____________________
4. Which sound is the softest? ____________________
5. Do you think that sounds can change categories? Explain your answer. ________

____

____

____

Make enough copies of this work sheet so that each student can have his/her own copy.

Clear As Glass

This Project

In this project your students will work with a variety of objects that are either transparent, translucent, or opaque. They will explore the ways in which light is transmitted, absorbed, or reflected when it strikes an object. A simple painting will be created, and the various ways in which light is transmitted (or not transmitted) will be identified.

Computer Skills

- painting
- paint mode
- text frames

Before Beginning

- Students should be familiar with how light reacts when it hits an object. They should know that when light passes through the object, it is being transmitted. Light can be transmitted through either transparent or translucent objects.
- Students should know that when an object does not let light pass through it, the object is opaque. An opaque object can either absorb or reflect light.
- Use the work sheet on page 74 to identify some objects as opaque, transparent, or translucent.

Quick Steps

- Open a new *ClarisWorks* painting document.
- Select an ***Opaque*** paint mode.
- Paint two large, red circles at the top of the screen.
- Select a ***Transparent*** paint mode. Change the fill color to white.
- Paint two smaller circles that overlap the bottoms of the red ones.
- Select a ***Tint*** paint mode. Keeping the fill color at white, paint a circle that overlaps the tops of the circles that were drawn.
- Label each of the circles as either opaque, transparent, or translucent.
- Save your painting with the file name *Colors.*
- Print a copy of your painting.

Clear As Glass *(cont.)*

Step 1 Open a new *ClarisWorks* document. Click on the ***Painting*** document. Click on the **OK** button.

Step 2 Pull down the **OPTIONS** menu and select ***Paint Mode***. Click in the small button next to the word ***Opaque***. Click on the **OK** button.

Step 3 Move the mouse to the tool bar and select the *oval* painting tool.

Step 4 Hold the mouse button down as you point to the Paint fill palette. Select a red paint.

Step 5 Bring the mouse back to the painting screen until the crosshairs are at the left side near the top of the screen.

Step 6 Hold down the mouse button as you drag the mouse to the right and then down, making a circle that is about 2 inches (5 cm) across.

If you want to paint an exact circle instead of an oval, hold the shift key down as you drag the mouse.

Step 7 Paint another red circle to the right of the first one. Leave a space of about .75 inch (2 cm) between the two circles.

Step 8 Pull down the **OPTIONS** menu and select ***Paint Mode***. Click in the small button next to the word ***Transparent***. Click on the **OK** button.

Step 9 Move the mouse to the tool bar and select the *oval* painting tool.

Step 10 Hold down the mouse button as you point to the Paint fill palette. Select a white color to paint with.

Step 11 Bring the mouse back to the painting screen until the crosshairs are at the bottom right side of the first circle, about 1/3 of the way into the circle.

If you do not like the position where the circle has been painted, pull down the **EDIT** menu and choose ***Undo Paint***. This will erase the last circle that you have painted.

Step 12 Paint another small circle at the bottom left portion of the second red circle. These two small circles should meet each other in the space between the two larger circles.

Step 13 Pull down the **OPTIONS** menu and select ***Paint Mode***. Click in the small button next to the word ***Tint***. Click on the **OK** button.

Step 14 Move the mouse to the tool bar and select the *oval* painting tool.

Clear As Glass *(cont.)*

Step 15 Hold down the mouse button as you point to the Paint fill palette. Select a white color to paint with.

Step 16 Paint another circle that overlaps each of the ones that you have previously drawn. You may have to try a few different placements until you get this circle in exactly the right position.

Step 17 Click on the Text tool in the tool bar. Place the crosshairs near the top of the screen. Hold down the mouse button as you drag the mouse across, creating a text frame. Type the word, *Opaque*.

Step 18 Return to the tool bar and select the *Straight line* tool. Bring the pointer arrow to the line width palette and choose a line width of ***3 points***.

Step 19 Click on the arrows palette and select ***Arrow at End***.

Step 20 Bring the crosshairs to just below the word "Opaque." Hold down the mouse button as you drag the mouse, drawing a line from the word to one of the large, red, opaque circles.

Step 21 Repeat Steps 17–20 to create labels for the transparent and translucent portions of the circles.

Step 22 Pull down the **FILE** menu and select ***Save As***. Give your painting the file name *Colors*. Click on the **Save** button.

Step 23 Pull down the **FILE** menu and select ***Print***. Click on the **Print** button. Although this project will look better if you print it on a color printer, you will still be able to see the different ways that light may be transmitted in a black and white or gray scale printing.

Step 24 Create a new *ClarisWorks* painting document and be creative. Make a picture that combines opaque, transparent, and translucent colors.

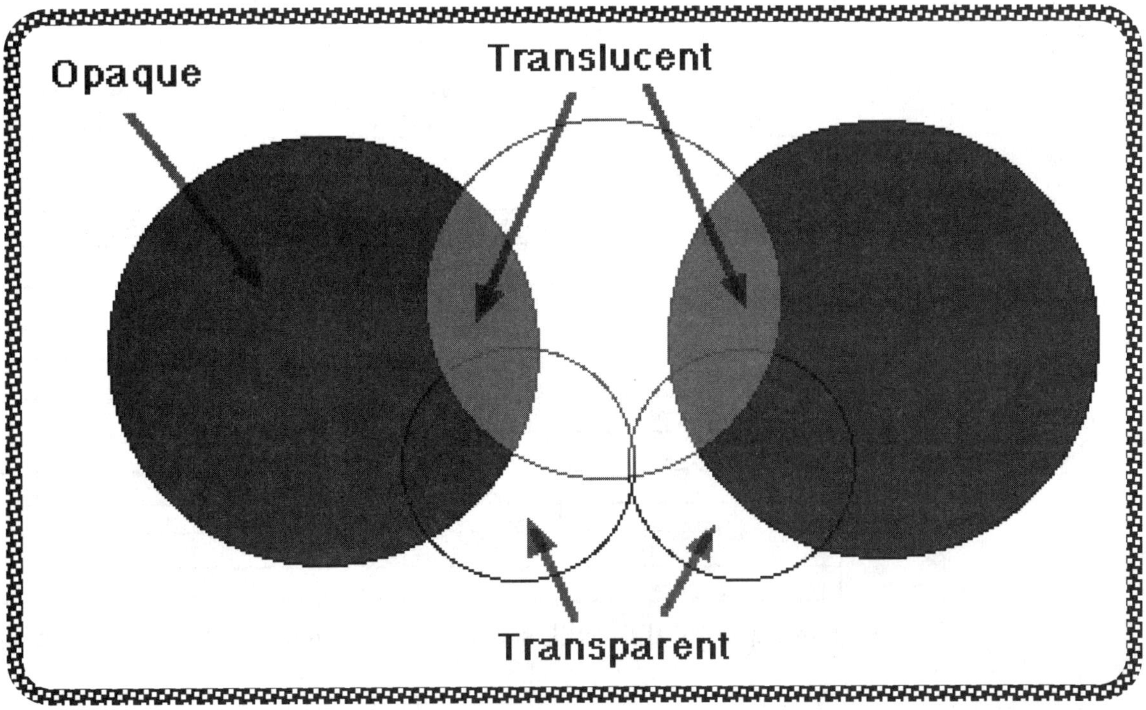

Clear As Glass *(cont.)*

Work Sheet

Match these drawings with the proper definition:

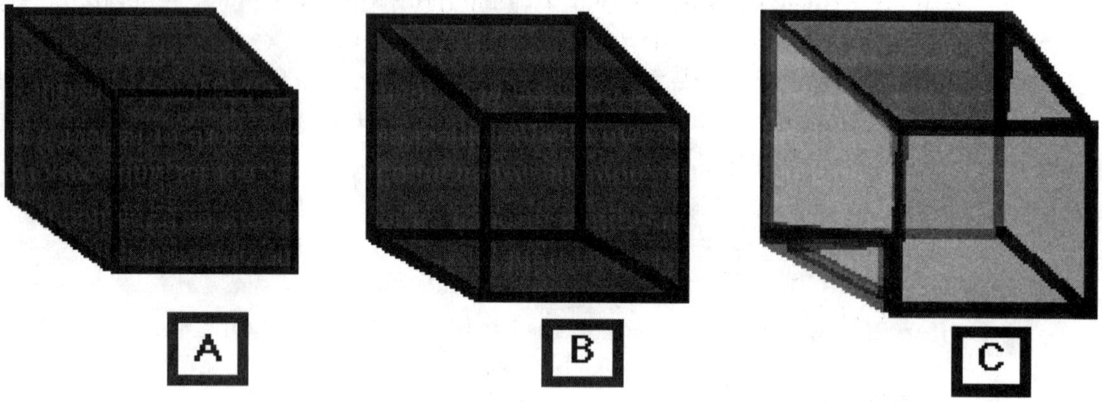

________ When light hits this object, it is transmitted through it. This substance is called **transparent**.

_______ When light hits this object it goes through it, but it is unclear and lacks detail. The colors look fuzzy. This substance is called **translucent**.

_______ When light hits this object it does not pass through it. Some colors are absorbed, while others are reflected off of it. This substance is called **opaque**.

Complete this chart by filling in the missing spaces. Add some items that you see around you every day.

Object	How Light Reacts to It	Color that is Reflected
Water		
Wood		
Waxed paper		
Looseleaf paper		
Frosted glass		
Clear glass		
Apple		
One blade of grass		

Make enough copies of this work sheet so that each student can have his/her own copy.

Sunlight Survey

This Project

What is the relationship among the hours of sunlight, the time of year, and the location on the globe? In this project students survey how long the sun is up at various places around the world. First, they must calculate the information from the sunrise/sunset figures they have obtained. Next, they chart and graph the data. Finally, they analyze the information and draw conclusions.

Computer Skills

- spreadsheet
- entering data
- graphs

Before Beginning

- Students should be aware of why different locations have different amounts of sunlight at various times of the year.
- Locate a resource for finding the time of sunrise and sunset for your city and three other cities around the country. You might look in the newspaper or on the World Wide Web. Try doing an Internet search for "sunrise sunset."
- Use the work sheet on page 78 to calculate the number of hours of sunlight for these locations.

Quick Steps

- Open a new *ClarisWorks* spreadsheet document.
- In cell A1 type in the title for this document, *Hours of Sunlight*. Make this cell 14 points and bold.
- Type the word "City" in cell A4. Make the cell bold and underlined.
- Enter the first date from the work sheet on page 78 into cell B3.
- Enter all of the dates for which you have recorded data in the cells in row B.
- Make this row bold and underlined.
- Enter the names of the cities for which you have gathered information in column A.
- Record the information from your work sheet into the appropriate cells.
- Make a line graph that displays the information in your chart.
- Save and print the file.

Sunlight Survey *(cont.)*

Step 1 Open *ClarisWorks* and click on **Spreadsheet**. Click on the **OK** button.

Step 2 Move the mouse until it points to cell A1. Click the mouse button to make this the active cell. Type the name of this spreadsheet, *Hours of Sunlight,* into the entry bar. Press return or enter to place the information into the active cell.

Step 3 Make A1 the active cell again. Pull down the **FORMAT** menu and select ***Size***. Make this cell ***14 point***.

Step 4 Choose Style from the **FORMAT** menu and select ***Bold***.

Step 5 Adjust the size of cell A1 by dragging the guide lines that are after and below the row and column names. When the pointer arrow is in the correct place to do this it will become a double arrow. Hold the mouse button down as you drag the line until all of the text shows.

Place the double-arrow pointer on the line beneath the row name marker (the number) for the row whose size you want to adjust. Double-click the mouse button, and the computer will automatically adjust the height of the cells in that row so that the largest item in the row fits into it. You can also adjust the width of a column by double-clicking on the guideline that is after the column name marker (the letter).

Step 6 Move the mouse so that it is pointing to cell A4. Click the mouse button to make this the active cell.

Step 7 Type the word *City* in the entry bar. Press return or enter to place the information into the active cell.

Step 8 Adjust the way this cell looks by pulling down the **FORMAT** menu. Make the Style ***Bold*** and ***Underlined.***

Step 9 Move the mouse so that it is pointing to cell B3. Click the mouse button to make this the active cell. Enter the first date from your work sheet on page 78. Press return or enter to place the information into the active cell.

Step 10 Adjust the way this cell looks by pulling down the **FORMAT** menu. Make the Style ***Bold*** and ***Underlined.***

Step 11 Continue to enter all of the dates from your work sheet into the cells in row B.

Step 12 Move the mouse until it is pointing to cell A5. Click the mouse button to make this the active cell. Type the name of the first city on the chart in your work sheet. Press return or enter to place the information into the cell.

Step 13 Enter all of the cities that are listed on your work sheet into column A. Remember to press return or enter after each entry to place the information into the active cell and make the cell beneath it the new active cell.

Sunlight Survey *(cont.)*

Step 14 Move the pointer to cell B5. Click on the mouse button to make it the active cell. Type the number of sunlight hours (this information is found on your work sheet) for the first city on the first date. Press return or enter to place the information into the cell.

Step 15 Record all of the information from your work sheet into the appropriate cells of the spreadsheet. Always remember to select the active cell by clicking the mouse button in it before you enter any information.

Step 16 Pull down the **FILE** menu and select ***Save As***. Name the file *Sunlight Survey*. Click on the **Save** button.

Step 17 To make a line graph of this information, click in cell A5, the cell that contains the name of the first city. Hold the mouse button down and drag the mouse until all of the information for all of the dates and all of the cities has been highlighted.

Step 18 Pull down the **OPTIONS** menu and select ***Make Chart***.

Step 19 Click on the **Line** button.

Step 20 Click on the **Axes** button. Click in the circle next to the Y-axis. Type *Hours of Sunlight* in the box for the axis label.

Step 21 Click on the **Axes** button. Click in the circle next to the X-axis. Type *Dates* in the box for the axis label.

Step 22 Click on the **Labels** button. Adjust the way the legend will look. Try a few options to see what you like.

Step 23 Type in a name for this graph. Adjust the way the title will look.

Step 24 Click on the **OK** button.

Step 25 Adjust the position of the graph on the spreadsheet page so that it is not blocking any of your data. Click on the graph so that the object is selected. Hold down the mouse button and drag it to a good place. You can also change the size of the graph by dragging one of the corner handles.

Step 26 Pull down the **FILE** menu and select ***Save As***. Keep the existing file name. Click on the **Save** button. Yes, you do want to replace the existing file.

Step 27 Pull down the **FILE** menu and select ***Print***. Click on the **Print** button.

Sunlight Survey *(cont.)*

Work Sheet

This chart shows the number of hours of sunlight at various places around the world in four different months. What information about the locations can you deduce from this information? Can you tell which location could be New York City? What location is near the Arctic Circle? What do we know about location #1? Where do you think location #2 can be found?

Sunlight Around the Globe				
	Hours of Sunlight			
Location	March	June	Sept.	Dec.
1	0	0	24	24
2	12	12	12	12
3	12	15	12	9
4	24	24	0	0

Use this chart to record the times that the sun rises and sets in the cities that you have selected for this project. Begin with your own city, listing the times of sunrise and sunset. Continue for three additional places. Calculate the amount of time during which there is daylight. Round your answer to the nearest quarter hour. Use the information from this chart to enter data on the spreadsheet that you created for your Sunlight Survey.

City ____________

Date	Sunrise	Sunset	Daylight Hours

City ____________

Date	Sunrise	Sunset	Daylight Hours

City ____________

Date	Sunrise	Sunset	Daylight Hours

City ____________

Date	Sunrise	Sunset	Daylight Hours

How Am I Doing?

This Project

Empower your students. Let them be aware of how they are doing in class. Each child will prepare his/her own grade book. They will be responsible for recording the grades that they get on tests and assignments. With this system, they will know what their averages are and in what areas they should be putting more effort.

Computer Skills

- spreadsheet
- entering data

Before Beginning

- This project enables your students to find their average grades. They should be aware of what an average is and how one finds the average of a series of numbers.
- For this project, your students will not be computing their averages; the computer will do the work for them. They will learn firsthand how technology can get work done faster and easier.
- The Student Activity Card on page 83 can be used to practice solving word problems using a spreadsheet.
- Use the Teacher Task Card on page 81 to prepare a template for this project.

Quick Steps

- Open the file called *How Am I Doing*?
- Add your name to cell B2.
- When your teacher returns a graded paper to you, enter the grade in the next cell in the correct column. Your average for that subject will appear in the Average Grade row.
- Save the file with the file name *My Grades.*
- Print your file to see how you are doing.

How Am I Doing? *(cont.)*

Step 1 Open *ClarisWorks* and click on the **Cancel** button.

Step 2 Pull down the **FILE** menu and select ***Open***. Click the mouse on the file called *How Am I Doing*?

Step 3 Move the mouse to cell B2 and click the mouse button. Move the mouse until the I-beam is in the entry bar. Click the mouse to place the cursor in front of the word "Grades." Type in (your name)'s. Press the return or enter key to move the information from the entry bar to the active cell.

Step 4 This grade book will be used to record the grades that you receive in your different subjects. Notice how each subject has its own column. When you receive a paper that has been graded, click the mouse in the next row of that subject's column.

In the sample spreadsheet on page 82, Spelling is in column A and Vocabulary is in column B. In what column is Math? ______ Science? _______ Social Studies? _______

Step 5 When the correct cell is selected, it becomes the active cell. Type the grade on your paper in the entry bar. Press the return or enter key to move the information from the entry bar to the active cell. Your average for that subject will appear in the Average Grade row (row 14).

Step 6 Pull down the **FILE** menu and select ***Save As***. Replace the current file name with the name *My Grades*. Click on the **Save** button.

Step 7 Pull down the **FILE** menu and select ***Close***.

When you receive another test or paper from your teacher, remember to enter the grade. This spreadsheet will help you see just how you are doing in all of your classes.

How Am I Doing? (cont.)

Teacher Task Card

Before your students begin to keep their own electronic grade books, prepare this spreadsheet that they will use as a template.

Step 1 Open a new *ClarisWorks* file and click on the **Spreadsheet** button. Click on the **OK** button.

Step 2 Click the mouse in cell B1 and type *How Am I Doing?* in the entry bar.

Step 3 Pull down the **FORMAT** menu and select ***Size***. Choose ***14 points***.

Step 4 Pull down the **FORMAT** menu and select ***Style***. Choose ***Bold***. Press the return or enter key to move the information from the entry bar to the active cell.

Step 5 Click the mouse in cell B2 and type *Grades*. Adjust the font size and style to be 12 points and bold.

Step 6 Click the mouse in cell B4 and type *Spelling*. Press the return or enter key to move the information from the entry bar to the active cell.

Step 7 Use cells C4, D4, etc., as you continue to enter the subjects for which you want your students to record their grades.

Step 8 Click the mouse in the #4 row marker box at the left side of the screen to select the entire row. Make these subject headings 12 points, bold, and double underlined. Press the return or enter key to move the information from the entry bar to the active cell.

Step 9 Adjust the size of each row and column so that the entire headings fit into the cell.

Step 10 Click the mouse in cell A14 and type the heading *Average Grade*. Make this entry bold and 12 points. Confirm the entry.

Step 11 Make cell B14 the active cell by clicking the mouse button in it. Pull down the **EDIT** menu and select ***Paste Function***. Choose the function for finding averages, [=AVERAGE(*number1*, *number2*, . . .)].

Step 12 This formula in now in the entry bar. Drag the mouse over the words "number1, number2, ..." When they are highlighted, click the mouse in cell B5 and drag it to cell B13. Notice how this range of cells in now listed in the entry bar. Press the return or enter key to move the information from the entry bar to the active cell.

You could choose to type in the range of cells that you want to average, but it is a lot easier to let the computer do the work for you.

You will see an error message in cell B14 (#NUM!), but do not worry. The computer is trying to average all of the grades in column A, but there is nothing with which to work. Once a grade has been entered, the error message will be replaced with the average.

How Am I Doing? (cont.)

Step 13 Click in cell B14 and drag the mouse until cell F14, or until you reach the last column that you have used. With these cells selected, pull down the **CALCULATE** menu and choose ***Fill Right***. The formula for averages that was placed in cell B14 will be copied to all of the selected cells in row 14.

Although the formula is copied from cell B14, the numbers that will be averaged for each column are those that are located in each individual column.

Step 14 Pull down the **FILE** menu and select ***Save As***. Replace the current file name, Untitled 1, with *How Am I Doing*? Click in the circle next to **Stationery**. Click on the **Save** button.

Step 15 Pull down the **FILE** menu and select ***Close***.

Your spreadsheet template is ready for your students to use. All that they have to do is open the file, add their names, and enter their grades. The computer will give each child his/her own grade report.

	A	B	C	D	E	F
1		How Am I Doing?				
2		Carrie's Grades				
3						
4		Spelling	Vocabulary	Math	Science	Social Studies
5						
6						
7						
8						
9						
10						
11						
12						
13						
14	Average Grade	#NUM!	#NUM!	#NUM!	#NUM!	#NUM!
15						

How Am I Doing? *(cont.)*

Student Activity Card

- Open the spreadsheet file called *How Am I Doing?*
- Use the information from this story to enter Carrie's grades into the spreadsheet.
- Save the file with the file name *Carrie's Grades.*
- Answer the questions below the story. The information that you will need can be found in the Carrie's Grades spreadsheet that you have just completed.

At the end of the first week of school Carrie had a spelling test. Spelling is not Carrie's best subject. In fact, it is her worst area. Although she studied for the test, Carrie only got a 70 on the test. She also had a math test. Now math is a subject where Carrie does very well. She got a 90 on the math test.

During the second week, Carrie practiced her spelling words every night. When she took the spelling test, her grade improved by 10 points. She was very happy. Carrie's math grade went up by five points too.

Carrie did not feel very well on testing day of the third week. Her test scores showed this. She got a 70 on her spelling test. Even her math score went down. She got an 85 on her math test.

The fourth week was a winning week for Carrie. She got a 90 on the spelling test and a 100 on the math test. These grades made Carrie very proud of herself.

What was Carrie's spelling grade average? _____%

What was Carrie's math grade average? _____%

What grade does Carrie need on her next spelling test to make her average greater than 80%? _____%

What grade does Carrie need on her next math test to make her average less than 90% _____%

Make enough copies of this work sheet so that each student can have his/her own copy.

Pattern Platter

This Project

Your students will enhance their critical thinking skills as they explore patterns. In this project students will be asked to examine patterns. They will look at the components of a pattern, how patterns repeat themselves, and how they can be duplicated. Students will challenge each other to match a pattern and predict what will come next.

Computer skills

- drawing
- rotating objects
- grouping objects
- copy and paste

Before Beginning

- Your students should be able to identify attributes of objects and see how they can impact on changes in a pattern.
- Use the work sheet on page 87 to help your students identify patterns and place them in groups.
- Use objects around the classroom to create patterns, for example, books, pens, pencils, chalk.
- What patterns and sequences do we find in our lives every day?

Quick Steps

- Open a new *ClarisWorks* drawing document.
- Create a text frame and write *Complete these patterns.*
- Draw a rectangle that is about 1 inch (2.5 cm) wide and .5 inch (1.3 cm) high.
- Copy the shape and paste it next to the first one. Fill the second shape with any pattern.
- Paste another copy of the first shape and paste it next to the second one.
- Rotate this shape 90 degrees so that it is taller rather than wider.
- Copy and paste this shape.
- Fill the last shape with the same pattern as the second rectangle.
- Select all of the objects and align them.
- Group all of the objects so that they become one object.
- Copy and paste the grouped object. Place it next to the first object group.
- Move down the page to a new position and draw three more patterns.
- Save this file with the file name *Patterns.*
- Print the file and give it to a classmate to draw the remaining segments of the patterns.

Pattern Platter *(cont.)*

Step 1 Open a new *ClarisWorks* document. Click on **Drawing**. Click on the **OK** button.

Step 2 Click on the *text* tool from the tool bar. Move the mouse until the I-beam is back at the drawing area. Hold down the mouse button and drag it across the top of the screen, creating a text frame.

Step 3 Type the words *Complete These Patterns.*

Step 4 Choose the pointer arrow from the tool bar and click the mouse button on the text frame to select it. Drag the text frame to the top center of the screen.

Step 5 Do a text makeover on the title of this page.

Step 6 Click on the *rectangle* tool in the tool bar. Move the mouse back to the drawing screen. Hold down the mouse button as you drag the mouse to the right for about 1 inch (2.5 cm). Do not let go of the mouse button as you drag the mouse down the screen for about .5 inch (1.3). Release the mouse button. You have just drawn a small rectangle.

Step 7 Pull down the **EDIT** menu and select ***Copy***. This places the selected object (the rectangle) onto the computer's clipboard.

Step 8 Pull down the **EDIT** menu and choose ***Paste***. Another copy of the selected object is placed on the screen. Drag it until it is lined up next to the first rectangle.

Step 9 Click on the *fill pattern* palette on the tool bar. Select a pattern that you like to fill this second shape.

Step 10 Pull down the **EDIT** menu and choose ***Paste*** again. Drag this shape until it is next to the second one.

Step 11 Pull down the **ARRANGE** menu and select ***Free Rotate***. Place the X marker on one of the corner handles. Hold down the mouse button as you move the mouse in a small circle. Notice how the rectangle rotates as you move. When you have traveled 90 degrees, the rectangle will be standing up and will be taller rather than wider.

Step 12 Pull down the **EDIT** menu and select ***Copy***. Pull down the **EDIT** menu and choose ***Paste***. Another copy of the tall rectangle is placed on the screen.

Step 13 Click on the *fill pattern* palette on the tool bar. Select the same pattern that you used before to fill this last rectangle.

Step 14 Pull down the **EDIT** menu and choose ***Select All***.

Pattern Platter *(cont.)*

Step 15 Pull down the **ARRANGE** menu and select ***Align Objects***.

Step 16 Click in the small circle next to *Align Bottom Edges* (top to bottom) and *None* (left to right). Click on the **OK** button.

Step 17 Keep all of the objects selected. Pull down the **ARRANGE** menu and choose ***Group***. The entire pattern is now grouped together as one object.

Step 18 Pull down the **EDIT** menu and select ***Copy***.

Step 19 Pull down the **EDIT** menu and select ***Paste***.

Step 20 Drag the pasted object (pattern) so that it is lined up next to the first pattern.

Step 21 Begin to draw a new pattern about 2 inches (5 cm) down the screen. Try some of these techniques for adjusting the shapes that you have drawn: different shapes, freely drawn figures, fill patterns, fill colors, line widths, line patterns, line colors, rotated shapes, resized shapes (scaled by percent), flipped horizontally, flipped vertically.

Step 22 Draw two more patterns on the screen. Leave them incomplete.

Step 23 Pull down the **FILE** menu and select ***Save As***. Name the file *Patterns*. Click on the **Save** button.

Step 24 Pull down the **FILE** menu and select ***Print***. Click on the **Print** button.

Step 25 Exchange papers with your classmates so that they can try to complete and duplicate your pattern.

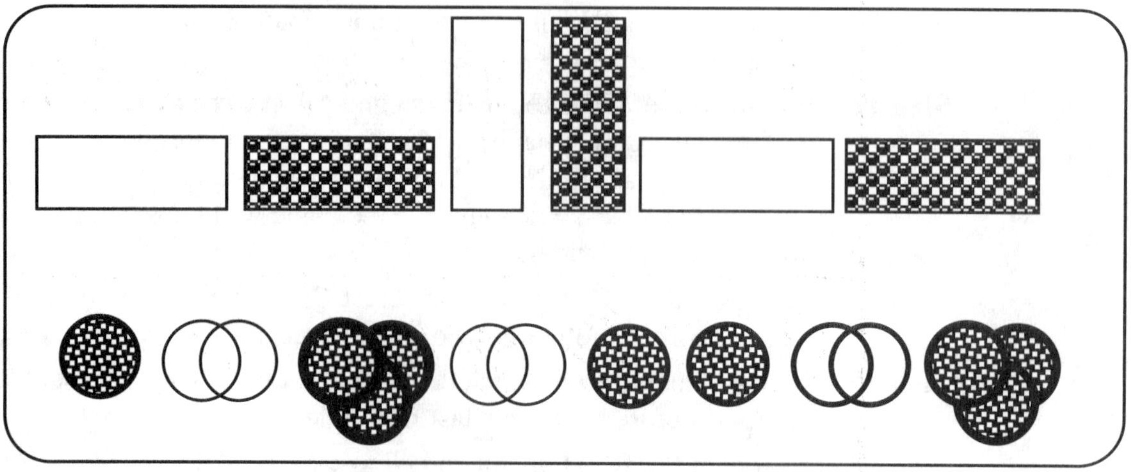

Pattern Platter *(cont.)*

Work Sheet

Identify the pattern in each sequence shown below. Draw a ring around one segment of the pattern. Complete the pattern if it is incomplete, or draw another segment if the entire pattern is showing. Answer the following questions for each pattern:

1. How many objects make up each segment of the pattern?
2. Draw a ring around any one object in the pattern. How many times does this shape appear in each segment?
3. If the pattern repeated itself 10 times, how many of these shapes would there be?
4. If the pattern repeated itself 25 times, how many of these shapes would there be?
5. If there are 150 objects in a series, how many complete pattern segments are there?

1 ________ 2 ________ 3 ________ 4 ________ 5 ________

1 ________ 2 ________ 3 ________ 4 ________ 5 ________

1 ________ 2 ________ 3 ________ 4 ________ 5 ________

1 ________ 2 ________ 3 ________ 4 ________ 5 ________

Homework Helper

This Project

This project is not limited to homework alone. Use the handy spreadsheet to check computational skills. Your students will be able to verify the answers that they have generated to problems involving the conversion of numbers from fractions to decimals and decimals to percents. This project is meant to be a way of checking work, not a means for doing it. It does not replace the need to learn how to make these conversions.

Computer Skills

- spreadsheet
- entering formulas
- entering data in cells

Before Beginning

- This project is used to check assignments. Your students need to have the skills that are needed to perform the necessary calculations before they use their Homework Helper. They should be able to convert a fraction to a decimal and change a decimal to a percentage.
- Use the work sheet on page 90 to practice these skills. The answers to the equations can be verified by using the Homework Helper spreadsheet.

Quick Steps

- Open a new *ClarisWork*s spreadsheet.
- Type *Homework Helper* into cell A1.
- Make the font ***14 points*** and ***Bold***.
- Enter the word *Numerator* into cell A3.
- Enter the word *Denominator* into cell B3.
- Enter the word *Decimal* into cell C3.
- Enter the word *Percent* into cell D3.
- Make row 3 ***14 points***, ***Underlined,*** and ***Bold***.
- Enter this formula for cell C4, = A4/B4.
- Make cell C4 ***fixed*** and ***2-place precision***.
- Enter this formula for cell D4, = C4
- Make cell D4 ***percent*** and ***2-place precision***.
- Save the file with the file name *Homework Helper*.
- Use this spreadsheet to help you check your class work and homework. Do not save the file when you are finished using it.

Homework Helper *(cont.)*

Step 1 Open a new *ClarisWorks* document. Click on **Spreadsheet** and then click on the **OK** button.

Step 2 Move the mouse until the spreadsheet marker is in cell A1. Click the mouse button to make this the active cell.

Step 3 Type the words *Homework Helper* into the entry bar. Press the return or enter key to move the information into the active cell.

Step 4 Click in cell A1 to make it the active cell again. Pull down the **FORMAT** menu and select ***Size***. Make the size of this cell ***14 points***.

Step 5 Pull down the **FORMAT** menu and select ***Style***. Make the style of this cell ***Bold***.

Step 6 Click the mouse in cell A3 to make it the active cell. Type the word *Numerator* in the entry bar. Click on the **Confirm Entry** box to move the words to the active cell.

Step 7 Click the mouse in cell B3 to make it the active cell. Type the word *Denominator* in the entry bar. Click on the **Confirm Entry** box to move the words to the active cell.

Step 8 Click the mouse in cell C3 to make it the active cell. Type the word *Decimal* in the entry bar. Click on the **Confirm Entry** box to move the words to the active cell.

Step 9 Click the mouse in cell D3 to make it the active cell. Type the word *Percent* in the entry bar. Click on the **Confirm Entry** box to move the words to the active cell.

Step 10 Click in the row heading box for row number 3, selecting the entire row. Pull down the **FORMAT** menu and choose ***Size*** and then select ***14 points***. Make the ***Style*** for this row ***Bold*** and ***Underlined***.

Step 11 Adjust the height of row 3 by placing the spreadsheet marker on the line between row headings #3 and #4. When a double arrow appears, drag the grid line until all of the words in row 3 can be seen. Adjust the width of the cells in each column by dragging the grid lines between the column headings until the entire word can be seen in each column.

Step 12 Click the mouse in cell C4 to make it the active cell. Type this formula into the entry bar, =A4/B4. Click on the **Confirm Entry** button to place the formula into the active cell.

Step 13 Double-click in cell C4. Click the mouse in the circle next to **Fixed** and type 2 in the box next to precision.

Step 14 Click the mouse in cell D4 to make it the active cell. Type this formula into the entry bar, =C4. Click on the **Confirm Entry** button to place the formula into the active cell.

Step 15 Double-click in cell D4. Click the mouse in the circle next to ***Percent*** and type 2 in the box next to precision.

Step 16 Pull down the **FILE** menu and choose ***Save As***. Give the file the file name *Homework Helper*. Click on the **Save** button.

Step 17 Enter the proper numbers to help you check your classwork and homework. Do not save the file when you are finished using your Homework Helper.

Homework Helper *(cont.)*

Work Sheet

This is what the Homework Helper spreadsheet looks like. To use it, type in the correct numbers for the numerator and denominator, and you will see what the equivalent decimal and percentage numbers are.

$$500 \div 750 = 500 / 750$$

Homework Helper			
Numerator	Denominator	Decimal	Percent
500	750	0.67	66.67%

Practice converting these fractions into decimals. Write the answers in the spaces provided. When you have completed all of the examples, open the *ClarisWorks* file called *Homework Helper*. Type in the correct numbers for the numerator and denominator. Is your answer the same as the one that the computer gives you?

33/99 = ______ 65/210= ______ 84/420= ______

75/425 = ______ 23/346= ______ 45/360= ______

18/72 = ______ 44/666= ______ 35/175= ______

60/580 = ______ 37/682= ______ 168/452= ______

Change these decimal numbers to percentages. Write the answers in the spaces provided. When you have completed all of the examples, open the *ClarisWorks* file called *Homework Helper*. Type the decimal in the correct column. Is your answer (percent) the same as the one that the computer gives you?

.4563 = ________% .3567 = ________% .9738 = ________%

.567 = ________% .865 = ________% .298 = ________%

.694 = ________% .908 = ________% .4860 = ________%

.051 = ________% .085 = ________% .0684 = ________%

Make enough copies of this work sheet so that each student can have his/her own copy.

Reading Relay

This Project

In this project your students will use a spreadsheet to record how many books they have read. Each student will have a target number to reach. As he/she approaches his goal, the number of books remaining to be read will be shown. A graph will be used to note the progress that the class is making.

Computer Skills

- spreadsheet
- using formulas
- making a line graph

Before Beginning

- Discuss the parameters for this project. How many books should each student read? What is a good goal to set for your class? What type of books should be read? Where will the books be read? How will a reading be verified? Set up rules and procedures that work well for you and your class. The reading log on page 94 of this book will be useful in keeping a record of the number of books that each student has read.
- Follow the directions on the Teacher Task Card on page 93 to prepare the spreadsheet for this project.

Quick Steps

- Open the *ClarisWorks* file called *Reading Relay.*
- Enter the number of books that you have read in the correct cell.
- Make a line graph that compares the number of books that you have read with five other students in your class.
- Save the file with the file name *Reading Relay.*
- Print a copy of the spreadsheet and graph.
- Update the spreadsheet whenever there is new information.

Reading Relay *(cont.)*

Step 1 Open *ClarisWorks* and click on the **Cancel** button. Pull down the **FILE** menu and locate the file called ***Reading Relay***. Click on the file name and then click on the **Open** button.

Step 2 Find the cell in column B that is in the row with your name. Move the mouse until the spreadsheet icon is in that cell and then click the mouse button to make it the active cell.

Step 3 Type the number of books that you have read into the entry bar.

Step 4 Click on the **confirm entry** button to move the information into the active cell.

Step 5 Move the mouse to the column A cell that has your name. Hold down the mouse button as you drag it to column B and then down for five more rows. When you release the mouse button, six cells in rows A and B will be highlighted.

Step 6 Pull down the **OPTIONS** menu and select ***Make Chart***. Click on the **Line** button.

Step 7 Click on the **Axes** button. Click the mouse in the small circle next to ***X-axis***. In the box next to axis label type *Names*.

Step 8 Click the mouse in the small circle next to ***Y-axis***. In the box next to Axis Label type *Number of Books*.

Step 9 Move the mouse to the box below the words Step Size and click the mouse button. Type the number 5.

Step 10 Click on the **Labels** button. In the box next to Title, type *Reading Relay*.

Step 11 Click in the small box next to Legend to deselect it. There should not be an X in the box. Click on the **OK** button.

Step 12 Pull down the **FILE** menu and choose ***Save As***. Click on the **Save** button. Yes, you do want to replace the original file.

Step 13 Pull down the **FILE** menu and choose ***Print***. Click on the **Print** button to print your graph and spreadsheet.

Continue to update this spreadsheet as you read more books.

Can you make a bar graph that compares the number of books that you have read to your target number? How would you graph a comparison of your own progress towards meeting your goal to that of a few of your classmates? **Hint:** The graph you draw is determined by the cells that you have selected.

Reading Relay *(cont.)*

Teacher Task Card

Use these directions to prepare the spreadsheet that your students will use to keep a record of their Reading Relay.

- Open a new *ClarisWorks* spreadsheet document. Click in cell A1 and type *Books That We Have Read.*
- Do a text makeover on this title. Pull down the **FORMAT** menu. Change the size to ***14 points***. Make the font, text color, and style whatever you want them to be.
- Click in cell A3 to make it the active cell. Type the word *Name* in the entry bar. Press the tab key to move to the next cell in the row.
- Type the following in each cell in row 3: *Number of Books*, *Reading Goal*, *Needed for Goal*.
- Find the row marker number for row 3 at the left side of the row. Click on it to select the entire row. Pull down the **FORMAT** menu and choose ***Size***. Make these words ***14 points***. Use ***Style*** to make them ***Bold*** and ***Underlined***.
- Pull down the **FORMAT** menu and select ***Alignment***. Choose ***Wrap***.
- Move the mouse until it is on the row markers between rows 1 and 2. You will see a double arrow. Hold down the mouse button, dragging it until all of the text appears.
- Adjust the height or width of each row or column so that all of the text shows. The column headings should appear on two lines.
- Click the mouse in cell A4 and type in one student's name. Press return or enter to move the information from the entry bar to the active cell.
- Continue to enter each of your students' names.
- Click the mouse in cell C4 and type in a reading goal for that student. Press return or enter to move the information from the entry bar to the active cell.
- Continue to enter a reading goal for each of your students.
- Click in cell D4 to make it the active cell. Type the following formula into the entry bar: =C4–B4.
- Click in cell D4 and drag the mouse down the column until it is in the row that contains the last student's name. All of the cells passed are now highlighted.
- Pull down the **CALCULATE** menu and choose ***Fill Down***. The formula from cell D4 is now copied into all of the selected cells.
- Move to the cell in column C that is a few rows below the last student's name. Type *Class Reading Goal* in that cell. Adjust the font to be larger, bold, and a color. Press return or enter to move to the next row in the column. Enter the words: *Books Needed to Meet Goal*. Do a font makeover for these words.
- Click in the cell next to the Class Reading Goal heading and enter the target number for your class.
- Click in the cell next to Books Needed to Meet Goal and type: = [Cell address] — *Sum*(B4.. [last student in row B]).

  Note: Only type the items that are in italics. The words in [] should be replaced with information from your own spreadsheet. Your formula will look something like this: =D31–SUM(B4..B29).
- Pull down the **FILE** menu and choose ***Save As***. Name the file *Reading Relay*. Click on the **Save** button.

Reading Relay (cont.)

Use this chart to keep a record of the books that you have read. After you have finished a book, prepare a summary activity for it. Your teacher will sign your chart if you can include the book in the Reading Relay spreadsheet.

Books That I Have Read

Title	Date Began	Date Completed	Summary Submitted	Approved to Enter in Chart

Glossary

Active cell—This is the cell in a spreadsheet where information will be placed. It is the cell that has been selected.

Align-on—This tab marker will set the tab spacing to line up with a specific character. It is often used with the decimal point to line up a column of numbers.

Browse—This mode enables you to look through a database. Let your mouse do the clicking as you browse through the records.

Carriage return—This occurs when [return] or [enter] is pressed. It sends the curser to a new line.

Cell—This is the place where information is held in a spreadsheet.

Cell address—Use this to know the exact location of a specific cell. It is formed by noting the intersection of the column and row.

Center align—This tab marker sets the tab spacing so that the words are centered on the position where the marker has been placed.

Clip art—Pre-drawn art work that can be placed in a document.

Column—In a spreadsheet, these are the vertical spaces. Columns are headed with letters.

Confirm entry box—Click on the little check box on the entry bar to move items from the entry bar to the active cell.

Crop—The process where parts of a graphic are removed or cut out.

Cross hair—A type of cursor that is used to define an area such as a text frame, graphics frame or a shape drawing.

Database—A document that is used to sort, organize and store information.

Default—These settings are automatic. If you do not make any different choices, this is what you will get.

Dialog box—This window appears when a selection has been made. It will ask you questions about how you want the computer to proceed in the activity that has been chosen.

Entry bar—This is the place where information is typed in a spreadsheet.

Field—In a database, this is a separate category where information is entered.

Fill down—When using a spreadsheet, this function copies the information (formulas or text) that is in the first selected cell to all of the selected cells in the original cell's column.

Fill right—This spreadsheet function copies all of the information (formulas or text) that is in the first cells of the selected column to all of the other selected cells in the original cell's row.

Frame—An area that allows you to use one type of ClarisWorks document within another type of document. For example, a text frame lets you write in a drawing document.

Grabber handle—The small boxes that appear on the sides and corners of selected graphics. These handles enable you to resize a selected item.

I-beam, Insertion beam—A marker that shows where text will appear on the screen.

Justified alignment—This is the alignment marker that arranges the text so that the text is placed in a straight line at both the left and right margins.

Glossary *(cont.)*

Left align—This marker arranges the text to form a straight left margin.

Locked cell—These cells cannot be changed. Information can not be added or removed.

Master page—In a drawing program, this feature allows you to create a template that will appear on each page of your document.

Object—An item that has been added to a document. It can be a frame or graphic.

Point—When the mouse is moved around the screen so that the pointer arrow is placed on an item.

Point size—This is the size of the letters that are typed.

Pointer arrow—The arrow that appears on the screen and moves when the mouse is moved.

Portrait—The position of a document on the paper is aligned so that the longer side of the page extends from top to bottom.

Record—In a database, this is the information contained in one set of fields.

Retrieve—Brings a file back to the screen that has previously been saved. This is the same as opening a file.

Right align—This marker arranges the text to form a straight left margin.

Row—In a spreadsheet, the row is the horizontal group of cells. Rows are named with numbers, .i.e., 1, 2, 3.

Ruler—These are the markings on the top of the screen that indicate tab positions, line spacing and alignment controls.

Search—When you are using a database, this function will allow you to look for records that meet the specified criteria.

Selection arrow—This tool is found in the tool bar. It is used when an item is to be chosen.

Sort—In a database, this function puts the records into a specific order.

Spreadsheet—A document that is used to crunch numbers and formulas.

Stationery—A way to save a file where, when it is opened, a new file is created with the text that you have previously entered. When you save the new file, the original remains the same. It is the same as a template file.

Style—The way that a font is set to look, i.e., bold, italic, underline.

Template—A way to save a file where, when it is opened, a new file is created with the text that you have previously entered. When you save the new file, the original remains the same. It is the same as a stationery file.

Tool—Icons that represent various objects that will help you while using your word processing program.

Tool bar—The pallet of tools that are available for use.

WYSISYG—Literally, What You See Is What You Get. This means that they way the text appears on the screen is the way that it will look when you print a hard copy.